Soviet MiG-15 Aces of the Korean War

SERIES EDITOR: TONY HOLMES

OSPREY AIRCRAFT OF THE ACES • 82

Soviet MiG-15 Aces of the Korean War

Leonid Krylov and Yuriy Tepsurkaev

OSPREY
PUBLISHING

First published in Great Britain in 2008 by Osprey Publishing,
PO Box 883, Oxford, OX1 9PL, UK
PO Box 3985, New York, NY 10185-3985, USA
Email: info@ospreypublishing.com

Osprey Publishing is part of the Osprey Group

Transferred to digital print on demand 2013

First published 2008
3rd impression 2009

Printed and bound in Great Britain

A CIP catalogue record for this book is available from the British Library

ISBN: 978 1 84603 299 8
PDF ISBN: 978 1 78200 886 6
ePub ISBN: 978 1 78200 850 7

Edited by Bruce Hales-Dutton and Tony Holmes
Page design by Tony Truscott
Cover artwork by Mark Postlethwaite
Aircraft profiles by Yuriy Tepsurkaev
Scale drawings by Leonid Krylov
Index by Alan Thatcher
Originated by PDQ Digital Media Solutions

The Woodland Trust
Osprey Publishing is supporting the Woodland Trust, the UK's leading woodland
conservation charity, by funding the dedication of trees.

www.ospreypublishing.com

Front cover
The battles fought between MiG-15s of 64th IAK and
Far East Air Force's Bomber Command in late
October 1951 were some of the fiercest, and
bloodiest of the entire Korean War. No fewer than
five Superfortresses were lost to Soviet fighters in
just 72 hours between the 22nd and 24th, with the
first of these being B-29A 44-61656 of the 19th Bomb
Wing. Its demise is depicted in this specially
commissioned artwork by Mark Postlethwaite, the
aircraft's destruction being credited to 12-kill ace Lt
Col Aleksander Smorchkov of 18th GvIAP. The Soviet
ace subsequently recalled;

'These B-29 missions were the most difficult I flew
in Korea. We took off in poor weather, and some of
my pilots had little experience of flying in such
conditions. We looked for breaks in the clouds, but
by the time we reached 10,000 m (32,500 ft) the sky
had become overcast. Then we received the order to
follow a course that would take us to the "big ones".
We had to lose 5000 m (16,000 ft) of altitude and fly
under clouds. But how could we find them through
the overcast? I could do it on my own, but I had the
whole regiment with me. I couldn't ask my base
because they would expect me to be able to
manage, and I might even be reprimanded for
asking such a question.

'I looked behind me and saw the whole regiment
there, holding formation well. I ordered them all to
put their noses down, to pay attention and not to
close up in the clouds. I could see my wingman but
nothing in front of me. I didn't want any collisions!
I was their commander, and therefore had
responsibility for all my pilots. If just one pair collided
it would be my fault. But we began to break out
of the clouds, and the overcast was above us.
And there they were – Superfortresses, just three
kilometres (two miles) from us. Our command post
estimated there were 12 bombers – I'd already
counted them – and up to 120 escorting fighters.

'What about my regiment? I looked around and
there they were! All of them were with me, and I felt
better at once. I ordered them to go for the big boys,
but not to forget the small ones. So we went into
the attack. The speed of our targets was 500 kmh
(312 mph) and ours was 1100 kmh (688 mph). The
escorting pilots appeared to be cowards. If we
forced them into a pair or a group of four aircraft,
they flew apart, right and left and left us a clear path
to the bombers. "Good", I thought. "These guys are
working for us". 'I fired a burst at one bomber and
saw my tracer rounds miss the target. As I got closer
I fired again at its right-hand engines and fuel tank.
Red flames came from them and the Superfortress
started to go down. As it began to break up, I saw six
parachutes opening, but there was no time for me to
watch, as the escorts seemed to have woken up.
'I had always taught my pilots that an aircraft like a
B-29 was worth all their ammunition. If each of us
could shoot down a Superfortress, then that would
be great. But I still had some ammunition left after
downing my bomber, so I used it to destroy an F-84.
I said to my wingman, Vladimir Voistinnyh, "Go
ahead and I'll cover you", as he went after a
Thunderjet, but the battle was fading away by
then and we were ordered home'.

CONTENTS

INTRODUCTION

The authors believe that any narrative about fighter aces of any air war should consider the way official combat scores match the actual losses suffered by the opposing side. No matter which air war is under discussion, the number of victories claimed by one side always significantly exceeds the losses actually inflicted on the enemy.

For the Soviet pilots involved in the Korean War, their superiors went to great lengths to verify such claims. Indeed, it took a long list of confirmations for a pilot from 64th IAK (*Istrebitelniy Aviatsionniy Korpus – Fighter Air Corps*) to be credited with victory in an aerial engagement. Returning from a mission, he would claim a kill by submitting a report to his regimental commander. This specified the time, place and direction of the attack, weather conditions at the time, results of the attack and the location of the crash site if the pilot saw the aircraft go down. Other pilots who had witnessed the event submitted similar reports.

The regimental photographic laboratory would also play a key role in securing a kill credit for the pilot, as its technicians developed camera gun film from the MiG-15 that showed the target under fire. A photo interpretation sheet based on the film was completed, and this contained entries for each frame – range to the target, target aspect ratio, target lead and evaluation of aim, whether unsatisfactory, satisfactory, good or excellent. It then indicated the percentage of frames showing good and excellent aiming and compared it with the amount of ammunition expended. A conclusion could then be drawn as to whether or not the enemy aircraft had indeed been shot down.

When the regiment had accumulated a sufficient number of claims, a search party was despatched to the area where the engagement took place to look for wreckage and to take corroborative statements from Chinese or North Korean authorities, as well as from ground troops. Every document obtained by the team was sent to the divisional HQ. In certain cases, intercepts of radio communications between enemy aircrew or search-and-rescue services could also provide confirmation.

Finally, if the divisional commander considered the evidence convincing, he would issue an order crediting the pilot with a kill.

In theory, such a procedure for registering victories seems reliable enough. Let us take a look at how it worked in practice, starting with the pilots' debriefing reports. The authors believe that such reports provided the most accurate and unbiased evidence of aerial victories, although in practice this was not

When wreckage such as this was found, there could be little doubting the validity of a claim made by a MiG-15 pilot following combat over North Korea. This section of fuselage skinning was from F-86E-6 52-2841 of the 4th FW's 334th FS, which was shot down by a Capt Smirnov on 6 October 1952. The pilot of the Sabre, 1Lt Myron E Stouffer Jnr, ejected and was captured

always so. It was extremely difficult, if not impossible, for a pilot to correctly evaluate the results of a combat action involving a rapid sequence of events. Obviously it would inadvisable for a pilot to watch an enemy aircraft under attack for too long. As a result, debriefing reports in which pilots stated they had seen an opponent crash were quite rare. In such circumstances, a damaged aircraft was often mistaken for one destroyed. This is well illustrated by the combat reports that followed three clashes between MiG-15bis fighters of 64th IAK and Royal Australian Air Force (RAAF) Meteor F 8s of No 77 Sqn.

On 29 August 1951, 15-kill ace Snr Lt L K Shchukin attacked Sqn Ldr D L Wilson in an engagement involving MiG-15s of 18th GvIAP (*Gvardeyskiy Istrebitelniy Aviatsionniy Polk* – Guards Fighter Air Regiment), 303rd IAD (*Istrebitelnaya Aviatsionnaya Diviziya* – Fighter Air Division) and RAAF Meteors. Rounds fired by the Soviet MiG pilot tore off the Meteor's port aileron and punched holes in its wing and rear fuselage. Shell fragments also riddled the main fuel tank. Apparently doomed, the Meteor rolled over and dived earthward. Yet Wilson managed to get his heavily damaged aircraft safely back to Kimpo, despite exceeding the Meteor's normal landing speed by 45 kmh (28 mph). The groundcrew repaired the aircraft, which operated for another five months before being shot down by anti-aircraft fire in February 1952.

On 5 September 11-kill ace Capt G U Okhay of 523rd IAP, 303rd IAD attacked a pair of Meteors. He fired two short bursts at the lead jet from a range of 350 m (380 yrd) and the latter started to descend. Okhay then fired a long burst at the wingman from 320 m (350 yrd). Wt Off W S Michelson lost control of his aircraft, which went into a dive from an altitude of 8000 m (26,000 ft). Due to damage inflicted to the tail of his fighter, Michelson had to be extremely careful in recovering from the dive. The Meteor levelled off at an altitude of about 3000 m (10,000 ft), having fallen five kilometres (three miles), but Okhay did not see this. He watched the Meteor fall to 5000 m (16,000 ft), after which he headed home as the order to land had been given almost five minutes earlier. Michelson managed to reach Kimpo and land successfully.

On 24 October 1951, 15-kill ace Maj Dmitriy Oskin of 523rd IAP saw a flight of Meteors during a dogfight with F-86s and engaged them from a range of 650-700 m (700-750 yrd). His target was piloted by Flt Lt P V Hamilton-Foster, and the MiG-15's rounds pierced the Meteor's port wing fuel tanks and starboard vertical stabiliser, damaged the fuselage and severed the elevator controls. The port engine also failed soon after Oskin had made his attack, forcing Hamilton-Foster to bank to port and dive away, his fighter billowing smoke. But again, despite the heavy damage, the Australian pilot managed to reach Kimpo. The remaining engine failed during Hamilton-Foster's final approach, but he was able to put the Meteor safely down on the runway. The Australian was recommended for the US Air Force's Distinguished Flying Cross for saving his aircraft.

These examples illustrate the difficulties pilots faced in making a correct assessment of the results of their actions during an aerial engagement. Indeed, aircraft that were not even damaged were sometimes thought to have been shot down. This was due to the superiority of the MiG-15bis in vertical manoeuvres compared with United Nations' fighters. This enabled Soviet pilots to break off combat

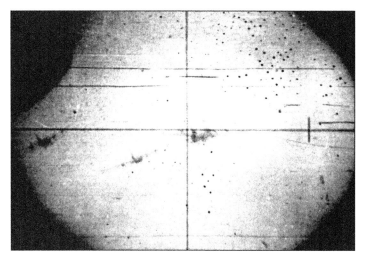

Gun camera film exposed by Snr Lt Obraztsov of 176th GvIAP, 324th IAD on 12 April 1951. It shows Obraztsov firing at a B-29 that is breaking out of the combat formation. The USAF announced the loss of three Superfortresses following attacks by MiGs on this date, with a fourth B-29 limping back to base and being declared damaged beyond repair. The quality of the photographs obtained by the MiG-15's gun camera remained poor throughout the conflict

by making a steep climb. Opposing aircraft, on the other hand, could usually evade the MiGs by diving.

It was not uncommon, therefore, for pilots to assume that an aircraft suddenly making a steep dive had been shot down. In this respect, it was easier for USAF pilots to assess their results over Korea – mortally damaged aircraft typically do not climb. But not all MiG pilots broke off combat by climbing when under attack. For example, on 8 November 1950, the world's first jet-versus-jet engagement ended when Snr Lt Kharitonov evaded Lt Russell Brown's F-80C by diving. Despite Kharitonov's MiG having sustained no damage whatsoever, Brown, from the 51st Fighter Wing (FW), claimed to have shot it down – he is still considered to have been the first pilot in aviation history to down a jet fighter in a dogfight.

The number of victories over B-29s claimed by 64th IAK pilots tallied with recorded losses suffered by Far East Air Force's Bomber Command for the most part. This did not always happen with claims made following dogfights with fighters and fighter-bombers, however. The large bombers normally flew straight and level, and one which made sudden and violent manoeuvres could reasonably be assumed to be about to crash – such evolutions were normal for fighters. Moreover, most pilots considered that when an opposing fighter flew straight and level, this was usually because the pilot had been incapacitated or the aircraft's control system significantly damaged.

Soviet pilots were also hindered in their ability to gain confirmation for their claims by the unreliability of the gun camera fitted to the MiG-15. Operating at a rate of only eight frames per second, the camera would stop immediately after the pilot had released his gun trigger. A normal cannon burst lasted about a second, and when the target was engaged from a range of 400-600 m (430-650 yrd) the camera stopped working just as the first rounds reached the target! If a burst was shorter or the range was longer, the camera failed to register the target at the moment the shells hit home.

The quality of the images taken by the camera was also affected by its rigid mounting, with frames often being blurred by the vibration caused when the guns fired. As a result, clear images of enemy aircraft being hit, burning or exploding in mid-air were rare.

Therefore, it was hard to confirm that a target had been destroyed based on the evidence presented on the photo interpretation sheet. In fact, the only reliable conclusion that could be drawn from most camera gun film was that a particular type of aircraft had been attacked from a certain range and angle. The unreliability of this film was demonstrated following the 20 May 1951 action involving Col E G Pepelyaev, regimental commander of 196th IAP, 324th IAD. In his debriefing report he claimed to have shot down a solitary F-86 in a dogfight, yet the photo interpretation sheet created following the examination of his gun camera recordings stated that he had achieved four kills! Pepelyaev was credited with a single victory, thus proving that the pilots' debriefing reports were considered to be more accurate and objective than the official photo interpretation sheets.

Confirmations based on eyewitness reports were similarly unreliable, as the following examples attest to. An intensive air engagement was fought over a bridge on the Chongchon River near Anju, involving pilots from three regiments of 64th IAK flying from three different airfields. During the dogfight, all three

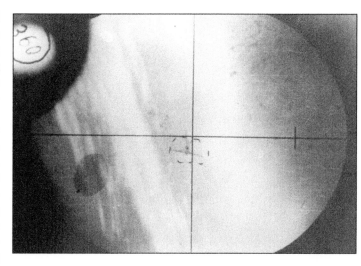

Gun camera film from the MiG-15 flown by Snr Lt Skorov (two Korean War victories) showing F-86E-6 52-2878 of the 51st FW's 16th FS being downed on 18 October 1952. Most western sources state that this aircraft was lost following an in-flight fire, but fail to note that the latter was caused by Skorov in his MiG! The Sabre's pilot, Capt Gabriel P Bartholomew, ejected and was captured

pilots attacked an enemy aircraft, noted the resulting hits and watched their opponents dive sharply away. They did not have time to follow them down, as they had to make further attacks and evade those of the enemy. Just one of the three jets attacked was destroyed, with the other two breaking off and returning home, despite suffering damage.

The crash of the only aircraft to be downed was observed by several pilots from all three regiments. Later, the pilots who had attacked enemy aircraft wrote debriefing reports independently of each other, and each claimed a kill. Their comrades who saw the aircraft crash confirmed the claims in their respective reports. The regiments then viewed gun camera film from the three pilots that scored hits, and this also confirmed the claims – target leads corresponded to the range and target aspect angle. As a result, one aircraft actually shot down became three claimed.

Later, three search parties were despatched to comb the combat area for wreckage. Since the regiments did not coordinate the work of their respective search parties, each left at its own time and followed its own route. All three subsequently arrived in the area near Anju one after another from different directions. Each turned to the nearest – and as it happened, different – police department, and one might have even consulted the headquarters of the nearest unit of the Chinese People's Volunteers or the People's Army of Korea. Irrespective of whom they consulted, they received positive answers when interviewees were asked if they had seen an enemy aircraft crash at a particular place, time and date. Such responses were made in writing, signed and sealed. Witnesses also specified the exact location of the crash site. Search parties, working independently of each other, then visited the site, took photos of the debris and removed data plates giving manufacturer's serial numbers.

It was not impossible for one of the search parties to find the wreckage of another aircraft previously shot down and mistake it for the one they had been looking for. In fact, a search party might not even reach the crash site, especially if it was in mountainous terrain. They might even conclude that there had been no crash at all, and that a mistake had been made. In this particular case, the proximity of water suggested that the enemy aircraft had sunk to the bottom of the Chongchon River, thus making it virtually impossible to determine whether it had crashed or not.

The presence of a large body of water so close to North Korea raised yet another possibility – that of an aircraft crossing the coastline in a steep dive but then crashing into the sea. Was the wreckage at the bottom of the sea or a nearby river, or did it manage to limp home?

Then again, the aircraft in question might not even have been hit at all, as the engine powering the F-86, for example, often trailed smoke, especially when at full throttle. It was easy to assume that a Sabre, diving steeply towards Korea Bay emitting smoke in an attempt to escape the attention of the MiGs, had been hit and was just seconds away from crashing. In such cases, reports from ground observers were not reliable. An aircraft flying at an altitude of 8000-9000 m (26,000-29,000 ft) could glide for a distance of 60-80 km (38-50 miles) with its engine shut down. And what if the engine malfunctioned but was still operating sufficiently enough to get the jet home?

The burnt-out tail section of Capt Bartholomew's F-86E-6 52-2878. Such wreckage was not always readily available to act as a source of confirmation for kills claimed by 64th IAK pilots in the heat of battle

The authors hope that the reader can appreciate the difficulties involved when it came to confirming a kill claim. Almost six decades later, an absolutely reliable confirmation system has still to be established. Yet in the case of operations over Korea in the early 1950s, the very inaccuracy of the system often meant that Soviet pilots were not credited with aircraft they had actually shot down. In some cases, victories were excised from combat scores because of insufficient confirmation.

The authors also believe that the following rule should be observed when assessing the results of aerial engagements, battles and warfare in general. Only the belligerents' actual losses should be considered, not the victories claimed by either side. It is, however, worth mentioning that the real loss picture is not always clear and obvious. USAF losses in Korea cited by various sources differ. For instance, a respected source states that one of the two Sabres lost on 6 October 1951 was downed in a dogfight with MiGs, the jet's pilot making an emergency landing on a beach when he found that he could not eject. Another source states that the F-86 was hit by anti-aircraft fire and crashed into the sea, while its pilot ejected. In this particular case the first source is correct – F-86A 49-1319, shot down by Col Pepelyaev, was recovered from the crash site and sent to Moscow.

In another example of inconsistencies in USAF loss records, officially, a B-29 downed by Yuriy Dobrovichan near the Suphun hydroelectric power plant on the night of 12 September 1952 fell to flak.

As a result of these anomalies, when discussing the achievements of specific pilots in aerial combat it is necessary to refer to official combat scores, even if they do not agree with losses admitted by opposing sides.

This rule holds true for the Korean War as much as for any other conflict before or since, and applies equally to the pilots of any nation. After all, most of them fought to the best of their abilities, and it is not their fault that a reliable way of confirming aerial victories has not yet been devised! The authors hope that readers of this book share this view.

COMBAT IN 1950

The People's Republic of China was proclaimed in December 1949, and on 13 February 1950 it signed a Treaty of Friendship, Alliance and Mutual Assistance with the Soviet Union, which included cooperation on matters of defence. Among other things, these provisions envisaged the USSR assisting China in establishing and training a modern air force – assistance that was expected to be provided by Soviet Air Force regiments stationed in China. At the same time, Soviet pilots were to provide air defence for key facilities until Chinese units gained sufficient expertise. Priority was given to the protection of Shanghai, then one of China's largest industrial and economic centres.

The Shanghai Group of Soviet Forces comprised 106th Fighter Air Division (IAD), which included 29th GvIAP (with 40 MiG-15s), 351st IAP (40 La-11s), 829th Combined Air Regiment (SAP, with 26 Il-10s and ten Tu-2s), an air transport squadron (ten Li-2s) and combat service support units. 29th GvIAP was based in Kubinka, near Moscow. Its flight and groundcrews arrived at Xuzhou on the evening of 3 March 1950. Regimental aircraft followed on 7 March, and within six days all 40 MiG-15s had become operational. By then, 351st IAP and 829th SAP had been flying from bases in the Liaodong Peninsula for almost a month.

On the night of 7 March, La-11s of 351st IAP flew to Xuzhou from Dalniy. The former was within the range of Nationalist Kuomintang (KMT) bombers, and Soviet fighters were required to defend the nearby MiG assembly site. 351st IAP started protecting the airfield, and a local railway station, the following day. On 13 March, Snr Lt Sidorov's flight detected a B-25 and shot it down 50 km (30 miles) from Xuzhou.

The following day, flight leader Snr Lt Dushin, whose aircraft were patrolling south of the airfield, detected another B-25. Dushin closed to within 50-70 m (55-75 yrd) and fired his weapons at the B-25's port and starboard engines. They caught fire and the bomber turned round and headed for the airfield, belly-landing four kilometres (2.5 miles) from Xuzhou. Six KMT crewmembers were captured, while the seventh was burned alive inside the aircraft.

On 17 March 19 La-11s of 351st IAP re-deployed to Shanghai's Jiangwan airfield to provide air defence for the city. Three days later, the unit encountered the enemy when a pair of La-11s intercepted two KMT P-51s. Insufficient air gunnery training prevented the Soviet pilots from exploiting their fighters' advantage, however, and the Mustangs went into a steep dive and crossed the coastline, taking them out of the Soviet fighters' area of operations.

Snr Lt Abramovich watches future ace Snr Lt A M Karelin conduct his pre-flight cockpit checks in an La-11 at Jiangwan airfield in 1950. Karelin, who would subsequently be credited with the destruction of six B-29s, did not achieve ace status until 28 January 1953

The 351st IAP's Snr Lt Dushin, who downed a B-25 over China and two B-26s over Korea, briefs a Chinese pilot at Jiangwan airfield in 1950

MiG-15s of 29th GvIAP are seen at Shanghai's Dachang air base shortly after they had flown in from Xuzhou on 1 April 1950. The jet in the foreground is MiG-15 0315367

MiG-15s from 29th GvIAP re-deployed from Xuzhou to the Shanghai Dachang air base on 1 April to boost the ranks of the Shanghai group of 106th IAD to 39 MiG-15s and 25 La-11s. The remaining 14 Lavochkin fighters from 351st IAP continued their patrols over Xuzhou, protecting the airfield and the nearby railway station. On 2 April a pair of La-11s flown by Capt Guzhov and Snr Lt Lyfar bounced two P-51s, and Guzhov shot both of them down.

829th SAP re-deployed from the Liaodong Peninsula to Xuzhou on 6-7 April, the ferry flight involving an intermediate stop at Qingdao. All the Ilyushin and Tupolev aircraft arrived safely at their new base.

A pair of MiG-15s led by Maj Keleynikov managed to intercept a photo-reconnaissance F-5E Lightning on 28 April, the KMT aircraft rolling over and diving away with its starboard engine on fire. Keleynikov was later credited with scoring the MiG's first kill in China, as radio intelligence had intercepted the Lightning pilot's distress call. Wreckage was duly found near an airfield on one of the Zhoushan islands.

Pilots of 29th GvIAP scored their second aerial victory after dark on 11 May. Capt Shinkarenko, leader of 4th Guards Squadron, intercepted a B-24J Liberator which was illuminated by searchlights. Closing in on the bomber, Shinkarenko fired three bursts and the Liberator went into a spin and crashed on the eastern outskirts of Shanghai. This proved to be the last aerial engagement fought by 106th IAD in China, as its combat operations officially ended in late July. The division then received a new assignment – training Peoples' Liberation Army Air Force units to fly Soviet-supplied aircraft. 351st IAP was to assist the Chinese 11th IAP in

mastering La-11s, while 29th GvIAP was to train 7th IAP to fly jets. Divisional flightcrews fulfilled these tasks until late October.

Meanwhile, on 26 September, the Shanghai Group of Forces ordered 106th IAD HQ, 29th GvIAP and certain combat service support units to re-deploy from Shanghai to Dalniy. 351st IAP and 829th SAP stayed behind to continue training the Chinese, however. A short time later, 106th IAD was re-designated 50th IAD, and in December 1950 it went into action in Korea. 29th GvIAP also fought in Korea as part of the division. 351st IAP was committed to the Korean War in September 1951.

CONFLICT IN KOREA

Shortly before daybreak on Sunday, 25 June 1950, North Korean forces invaded South Korea. Three days later the South Korean capital, Seoul, was captured and the UN sanctioned the despatch of military assistance, under US leadership, to repel the North Korean invaders.

The first US Army units – from the 8th Army – were committed to battle on 5 July. On 4 August North Korean troops reached the Nakdong River in the southeast corner of the Korean Peninsula, trapping UN forces in the Pusan Perimeter. Gen Douglas MacArthur, Supreme Commander of UN Forces in Korea, concentrated his forces inside the Pusan Perimeter for over a month, pending a counter-offensive. Finally, on 15 September, he ordered an amphibious landing at Inchon to take the North Korean troops in the flank. A week later he ordered the 8th Army to advance north from Pusan. By October, North Korean forces had been driven back behind the pre-war demarcation line formed by the 38th parallel of latitude. UN units reached the Yalu River, on the Korean-Chinese border, on 26 October.

When the Chinese government's warning that it would come to North Korea's assistance if the 38th parallel was crossed by non-South Korean units was ignored, its direct participation in the war became inevitable. During preparations for the resulting offensive, Soviet Air Force units in-theatre were tasked with providing air cover for the Chinese troops, their supply lines and for key points in the northeast of the country.

The key unit involved in supplying aircraft for these missions was 151st GvIAD of the Soviet Air Force based in Manchuria. From August 1950, three of its regiments – 28th, 72nd and 139th GvIAPs – were based at Anshan and Liaoyang airfields, near Mukden, where they trained Chinese pilots to fly jets and then to defend the northeast. In late October 151st GvIAD allocated personnel to form 67th IAP, which, together with 139th GvIAP, comprised the new 28th IAD.

At 1350 hrs on 1 November, 1st Squadron of 72nd GvIAP was ordered into the air. This unit was led by Hero of the Soviet Union (HSU) Maj N V Stroykov, who had flown 245 combat sorties in World War 2, fought in 66 air battles and had 16 personal and 21 group victories to his credit. Flying the MiG-15s in his formation on that day were Snr Lts Guts and Kaznacheev and Lts Monakhov, Chizh and Sanin. As it happened, only five MiG-15s took off because Sanin's was unserviceable. The others were told to head for Antung, on the Yalu River, close to the border with North Korea. When the group arrived here, it was ordered to cross the border, start hunting for enemy aircraft and attack any that were detected. The five MiGs headed southeast, deep into Korean territory.

At 1415 hrs Guts, leading the second pair, detected three USAF F-51D Mustangs. All five MiGs attacked simultaneously, but the American pilots initially managed to avoid a dogfight through some skilful flying. Two F-51s made sharp turns and one half-rolled, dived and headed south at full speed. According to Soviet documents, Chizh downed a Mustang during a second attack (USAF records state that no Mustangs were lost), while the third F-51 dived steeply and broke away to the south.

Four MiGs from 72nd GvIAP's 2nd Squadron left for Antung 26 minutes after Stroykov's group had arrived overhead the Yalu River, these aircraft being led by the squadron leader, Maj Bordun. Some 25 minutes later the MiG pilots were told to return to base by their ground controller, and they headed back to Anshan. However, less than three minutes later they received orders sending them back to Antung to repulse an enemy air strike that had just been reported by ground troops.

Maj Bordun, Snr Lt Khominich and Lt Sukhov altered course for the Korean border, while Lt Esyunin returned to base, as his jet was not fitted with external tanks – he was now running low on fuel. At 1550 hrs, Snr Lt Khominich spotted ten F-80C Shooting Stars ahead of him, and he attacked the leading group of four from out of the sun. He opened fire and peppered one of the F-80s with a three-second burst of cannon fire, ceasing when the range was down to 200 m (220 yrd). The Shooting Star was deemed to have been shot down by the Soviet pilots in what had been the first-ever dogfight between jet fighters.

The USAF admitted losing two F-80s on 1 November, one of which had been shot down by anti-aircraft artillery during a morning air strike on Sinuiju airfield. The second jet, from the 49th Fighter-Bomber Group (FBG), was listed as having been shot down on the afternoon of the 1st during a rocket attack near Unsan, but USAF records make no mention of the dogfight between the F-80s and the MiGs. Despite the Shooting Star pilot having been killed in the engagement, it is hard to believe that his squadronmates had failed to notice the attack by the Soviet fighters.

The archives on both sides are uncertain as to whether Khominich really did score a victory during this all-jet clash, with details about what caused the F-80's demise being unclear. Clearly a second Shooting Star was lost on 1 November, but where did it crash? Did it explode in mid-air or come down in the sea? Such questions still remain unanswered.

Pilots from 28th GvIAP also flew their first combat sorties on 1 November, but they did not encounter the enemy.

A further five days would pass before Soviet MiGs tangled with USAF aircraft once again. On 6 and 7 November several dogfights took place between 28th GvIAP aircraft and F-51s on ground attack missions, and the destruction of a single Mustang (there is no USAF loss that tallies with this claim) was shared between three MiG pilots. One of the latter was Maj V I Kolyadin, commander of 28th GvIAP and a HSU, who had claimed 15 victories in 30 aerial engagements during the course of 685 combat sorties in World War 2. He would subsequently become the second MiG-15 pilot to score five victories over Korea.

SUPERFORTRESS STRIKE

On the morning of 8 November, USAF fighter-bombers started preparing for a coordinated strike with 70 B-29s on Sinuiju and the nearby bridge over the Yalu. Throughout the Korean War this bridge would be a thorn in the side of UN forces, as it was used by the Chinese to transfer troops and military equipment in bulk into North Korea.

Some 90 minutes before the bombers' appearance, Mustangs and Shooting Stars attacked flak batteries on the Yalu River's left bank with bombs, rockets and machine gun fire. The B-29s, approaching at an altitude of 6000 m (20,000 ft), were in turn escorted by two flights of F-80Cs that had already attacked the flak batteries with bombs and napalm canisters. Just minutes before the B-29s dropped their bombs, the escorting fighter pilots sighted eight MiGs, split into two flights, approaching from the Chinese side of the river. The leading group of four Soviet fighters attacked Mustangs that were still strafing the flak batteries, while the second flight was itself attacked by F-80Cs from the 51st FW.

As briefly discussed in the introduction to this book, the ensuing dogfight has gone down in the history of combat aviation because it is believed in the West that during the engagement Shooting Star pilot 1Lt Russell Brown had become the first aviator to achieve a kill in a jet-versus-jet clash. Such an acknowledgement ignores the 1 November incident in which an F-80 reportedly fell victim to a MiG-15.

In any case, the covering group of four MiGs had to evade the F-80s' attack, instead of launching its own against the B-29s. Apart from Lt Kharitonov, who chose to dive, the remaining Soviet fighter pilots evaded the Shooting Stars by climbing steeply away. Brown, seeing Kharitonov's MiG passing below him, rolled and dived on his opponent. The F-80 was heavier than the MiG, and it accelerated faster in the dive. Brown caught the Soviet fighter in his crosshairs close to the ground and pressed the trigger, but only one of his six machine guns fired.

At that moment Kharitonov jettisoned his external fuel tanks in an effort to lighten his fighter. As thick haze limited visibility, blurring the outline of the MiG, Brown mistook the drop tanks for debris. No UN pilot had previously seen MiG-15s jettison their external tanks before – indeed, Kharitonov had just become the first Soviet pilot in Korea to do so during a dogfight. In fact, during the period of combat operations described in this chapter, the number of drop tanks carried by MiG-15s was limited, and thus each was considered to be worth its weight in gold. Pilots, therefore, had to put up with inferior flight characteristics for the sake of prolonging their stay in the combat area. This problem was later solved when hundreds of tanks were despatched from the Soviet Union. Eventually, a production line for drop tanks was also established in a series of Chinese factories located close to MiG bases.

The plumes of kerosene that trailed the tanks as they fell away from the diving MiG helped to reinforce the illusion that Kharitonov's fighter had been mortally hit. Brown had lost sight of what he believed to be a damaged aircraft in the haze close to the ground moments before Kharitonov had recovered from his dive at an extremely low altitude. But Brown saw dust and smoke coming up from the ground as the drop tanks hit terra firma, which he took for indications of his success. Yet at that very moment Kharitonov was already setting course for Anshan.

That same morning, pilots from 28th, 72nd and 139th GvIAPs claimed to have shot down three F-51s without loss to themselves – again, there are no official USAF losses that back these 'kills' up. And the MiG units failed to accomplish their most important task, as the Superfortresses bombed their targets unhindered. A total of 70 B-29s appeared over Sinuiju at an altitude of 6000 m (20,000 ft) 30 minutes after the fighter-bombers' attack had finished, and they dropped 580 tons of incendiary bombs on the city.

When the main force retreated, nine more Superfortresses made a pass over the city and attacked the Yalu Bridge, but the 454-kg (1000-lb) high-explosive bombs they dropped damaged only the road leading up to the bridge, rather than the structure itself. The Soviet fighters had failed to intercept the B-29s because they had received the word to scramble too late. By the time they reached Sinuiju, the MiG pilots saw only the tails of the withdrawing bombers, so there was no point in chasing them.

Despite having bombed the target unmolested, the results achieved by the B-29s failed to satisfy senior UN commanders. Much of Sinuiju had been burned to the ground, but the bridge over the Yalu remained intact. It would have to be attacked again over coming days, but this time by aircraft from US Navy carriers sailing off the coast of Korea.

On 9 November, RB-29A 44-61813 of the USAF's 31st Strategic Reconnaissance Squadron, escorted by two flights of Shooting Stars, was sent to the Sinuiju area to direct a strike by US naval aircraft. Once in the target area, the aircraft was attacked by two MiG-15s from 72nd GvIAP flown by Maj Bordun and Snr Lt Dymchenko. They made two passes at the RB-29, which caught fire and then dived at full throttle for UN-held territory. The Soviet pilots were credited with a joint victory. As it happened, the RB-29 crashed while attempting an emergency landing at Johnson Air Base, in Japan, killing five crewmembers.

Later in the day, MiGs from 139th GvIAP encountered F9F Panthers from USS *Valley Forge*, which they mistook for F-80s. Maj Aleksandr Stulov and Snr Lt Kaznacheev were each credited with downing a 'Shooting Star' (a solitary F9F was lost when it hit the landing barrier aboard *Valley Forge* upon returning to the carrier – none were shot down).

With no two-seat MiG-15s then available, Soviet units in China relied on aircraft such as this ungainly looking Yak-17UTI to introduce Chinese and North Korean pilots to jet aviation. This particular aircraft was assigned to 29th GvIAP at Dachang air base in 1950

US Navy AD Skyraiders and F4U Corsairs, escorted by F9F Panthers, attacked the bridge near Sinuiju once again on 10 November. Seven MiG-15s from 139th GvIAP and six from 72nd GvIAP were scrambled to intercept them, although the fighters from the latter regiment arrived too late to engage the enemy. 139th GvIAP's MiG pilots fought a fierce battle with both Skyraiders and Panthers, which they mistook for Thunderbolts and Shooting Stars. Fighter pilots from 139th GvIAP were credited with shooting down three 'F-80s' and an

Maj Aleksandr Stulov of 139th GvIAP, 28th IAD, seen here during World War 2, was credited with shooting down an F-80 on 9 November 1950

'F-47', although the only Navy aircraft lost according to official records was a Skyraider from VA-35 that crashed while landing aboard USS *Leyte*. But 139th GvIAP pilot Capt Grachyov was shot down by Lt Cdr William Amen, CO of Panther-equipped VF-111 embarked in USS *Philippine Sea*. It was the first loss suffered by Soviet fighter pilots in the Korean War, and also the first jet kill to be confirmed as destroyed by either side.

The MiGs were engaged in intensive combat operations for four more days, with Soviet pilots repeatedly encountering Superfortresses, Mustangs, Shooting Stars, Panthers and Skyraiders. As previously noted, the latter two types were usually mistaken for F-80s and F-47s. The MiG pilots were credited with downing five B-29s, five F-80s, two F-51s and an 'F-47' during these clashes, although these victories do not tally with UN losses. In return, a MiG-15 from 151st Division was lost when Snr Lt Nasonov of 28th GvIAP was killed in a dogfight with an F-80 on 11 November – no Shooting Star pilots made a claim on this day, however. Nasonov had fought in 28 aerial engagements and scored 12 victories during the course of 226 combat sorties in World War 2.

The weather deteriorated on 15 November, with much of North Korea being obscured by dense cloud cover. The airspace below the cloud base was usually obscured by haze and, on occasion, drizzle. Pilots from 151st and 28th IADs remained on combat duty at their respective airfields, but the weather prevented the enemy from being active. Poor flying conditions persisted until month-end, with Soviet pilots managing to get airborne just three times between 15 and 30 November.

The only action during this period took place on 18 November, when 14 pilots from 139th GvIAP fought 30 enemy aircraft that they again mistook for 'F-47s' and 'F-80s'. In fact, they had encountered carrier-based attack aircraft and their escorting Panthers. Capt Pakhomov and Lt Bulaev each reported shooting down an 'F-80' (no losses were reported by the US Navy). The MiG-15 piloted by the deputy squadron leader, Snr Lt Arkady Tarshinov, was shot down, although again there were no kills claimed by UN aircraft.

Three days prior to this action taking place, the commander of the Soviet Air Task Force in China, Lt Gen Krasovskiy, received encrypted cable No 5564 from the Chief of the Soviet General Staff. It contained the order for Krasovskiy to prepare a fighter air corps for combat operations in the Korean Peninsula as soon as possible – the new corps was to be designated 64th IAK. The force was established at Mukden between 15 and 24 November, with Maj Gen Belov being appointed corps commander.

On 21 November, 28th, 50th and 151st IADs were attached to 64th IAK, but 28th IAD did not fight as part of the corps for some time to come as in late November it was redeployed to a base near Qingdao to continue training Chinese pilots. The air regiments of 151st GvIAD were also kept busy performing this task. Both 28th IAD and 151st GvIAD remained off combat operations until February 1951, leaving 50th IAD, 29th GvIAP and 177th IAP to carry the fight to UN forces – MiG-15s from 50th IAD performed their first combat sortie on 30 November.

29TH GvIAP INTO ACTION

Having helped provide the air defence for Shanghai for much of 1950, 29th GvIAP and the HQ unit of 106th IAD were redeployed to Xiansilipu airfield in the Liaodong Peninsula in the autumn of that year. Their commanding division, 50th IAD, had commenced preparations for combat operations in Korea in October 1950. By then the division controlled both 29th GvIAP and 177th IAP, the latter having arrived from 303rd IAD – this division was to be committed to the conflict seven months later.

177th IAP and 29th GvIAP received new MiG-15bis fighters just prior to being committed to the action over North Korea. Having re-equipped, 50th IAD flew to Anshan on 20 November. Four days later, all divisional aircraft had their red stars replaced with North Korean Air Force markings ready for the fray.

On 1 December, six 50th IAD pilots performed the division's first combat mission over North Korea when they were scrambled to intercept B-29s detected near Antung. When they returned to Anshan, the Soviet pilots were only able to report damaging two Superfortresses, yet on the basis of camera gun data, Snr Lts Orlov and Grebenkin were each credited with kills (no B-29s were lost according to USAF records). Their victories were the first for both 29th GvIAP and 50th IAD in Korea.

A pilot from 29th GvIAP salutes his groundcrew as they stand to attention in front of MiG-15 0315372 at Dachang air base in 1950

In early December communist forces advanced southwards, and 50th IAD was tasked with protecting North Korean facilities and supply routes up to 75 km (50 miles) from the Chinese border. In reality, Soviet fighters would routinely intercept enemy aircraft at a considerably greater range – sometimes up to 120 km (75 miles) from the Yalu River – as crucial bridges and crossings over the Chongchon and Kuren rivers also had to be protected.

In order to perform these missions more effectively, 64th IAK decided to use Antung airfield, which was the closest base to the North Korean-Chinese border. Now, MiGs taking off from Antung could expand their area of operations as far as Pyongyang and further south. 29th GvIAP redeployed to the new airfield on 3 December, although 177th IAP stayed at Anshan. Antung remained the only forward airfield for 64th IAK fighters for some time to come, although new bases were eventually constructed around the city during the summer of 1951.

Soviet fighters made their first combat sortie from Antung at noon on 4 December 1950 when a flight of MiG-15bis, led by Guards Capt Vedenskiy of the 2nd Squadron, 29th GvIAP, was scrambled to intercept RB-45C Tornado 48-0015 of the 84th Bomb Squadron's Det A. The enemy reconnaissance aircraft was shot down near Anju, with two of its crew being captured and a third posted as missing in action.

Capt Stepan Naumenko, deputy leader of the 1st Squadron, 29th GvIAP, opened his combat score that same day. He would subsequently become the first Soviet pilot in Korea to achieve five kills. The three pairs of fighters under Naumenko's charge were scrambled to intercept two enemy aircraft detected near Antung – the contacts were soon identified as F-84s, and the MiGs set off in pursuit. The USAF aircraft dropped their external fuel tanks and tried to break off by diving at high speed, but the wingman lagged behind his leader. Naumenko accelerated to 1050 km/h (650 mph) and gradually caught the Thunderjet. Closing to a range of 600 m (650 yrd), Naumenko opened fire. The F-84 started to trail smoke and flames after the second burst, and it eventually rolled to the right and dived away.

Without slowing down, Naumenko then attacked the lead Thunderjet, which tried to break off after the first burst by rolling and climbing to port. The pilot then banked sharply to starboard, and Naumenko followed, firing two more short bursts from 400-500 m (430-550 yrd). His rounds set the F-84 alight. It too rolled to the right and dived towards the frontline. Naumenko was credited with downing both F-84s, although USAF records indicate that no Thunderjets were lost on this date.

Snr Lt Rumyantsev fell victim to the weak tail structure of the MiG-15bis during the course of this engagement, however. Turning sharply at high speed and low altitude as he attempted to stay with Naumenko during the dogfight, Rumyantsev perished when the MiG's elevators buckled under high-G loading and the aircraft went out of control and hit the ground before he could eject out.

Naumenko scored his next victory on 6 December whilst leading six MiGs that had been scrambled to intercept five B-29s. Several attacks resulted in two Superfortresses being set on fire, but the Soviet pilots were credited with three kills, one of them being attributed to

Naumenko – again, no B-29s were listed by the USAF as having been lost. Lt Serikov did not return from the mission, and it was presumed that he was downed by defensive fire from one of the bombers. No claims made by Superfortress gunners on this day were officially recognised as victories by the USAF, however.

ENTER THE SABRE

Following the early aerial clashes in December 1950, pilots of 29th GvIAP had been credited with shooting down five B-29s, one RB-45C, ten F-80s and six F-84s (most of these claims cannot be matched up with USAF losses) for the loss of three MiGs-15bis and their pilots. And only one of the latter had been downed by the enemy, with the rest having fallen victim to airframe malfunctions. Another MiG-15bis was heavily damaged in a dogfight with an F-84, but it was repaired by regimental groundcrews. The air superiority clearly enjoyed by the MiG units in November-December 1950 was about to change drastically, however, for on 10 December the first F-86A Sabres arrived in-theatre.

In an effort to counter the new fighter's effect on the balance of aerial power in-theatre, 177th IAP was posted to Antung on 15 December, with two more squadrons being sent to the base on Christmas Day.

The first clash between MiG-15s and F-86s, fought on 17 December, ended in the US pilots' favour when Lt Col Bruce Hinton of the 4th FW downed 50th IAD instructor pilot Maj Yakov Efromeenko. The latter, who was wingman to deputy regimental commander Maj Keleynikov as part of a four-aircraft group from the 29th GvIAP, was able to eject.

Although six MiGs took off on the 17th, only four of Keleynikov's fighters succeeded in reaching their patrol line, as the lead pilot in one of the jets was unable to retract his landing gear after take-off and had had to return to base with his wingman. Once over the Yalu River, the remaining Soviet pilots were alerted to the presence of unidentified aircraft when one of them called 'Four aircraft below!' over the radio. Then, after a short pause, they heard Efromeenko's voice. 'Those are friendly'. The next call came from the command-and-control post. '04, you are all alone, 04 you are all alone!' Then, silence.

Keleynikov's flight had, in fact, sighted two groups of aircraft, with the first being straight-winged F-80s or F-84s immediately below them – the MiG pilots commenced a gentle diving turn in order to intercept them. Four of the newly arrived Sabres were then spotted by Efromeenko, who had mistaken them for MiG-15s from 177th IAP. Right up to the time he was shot down, the Soviet instructor pilot thought he was being tailed by a MiG-15.

Soviet pilots encountered Sabres again on 19 and 21 December, and two MiGs were damaged. On the 21st, a 29th GvIAP pilot was credited with downing an F-86, although the

Combat veterans from the 3rd Squadron, 29th GvIAP, pose for a photograph soon after returning to the USSR from Korea in February 1951. They are, from left to right, Maj Perekrest (three Korean War victories), Capt Petrov (one victory), Snr Lt Nikitin, Capts Ryzhov (one victory) and Fedoseev (one victory) and Snr Lts Sotnikov (one victory), Polyakov and Bondarenko (two victories)

USAF did not admit losing its first Sabre until the following day. The victor on the 22nd was Capt Vorobyov, deputy leader of 177th IAP's 1st Squadron – he would claim a second kill later in the war.

Vorobyov was flying one of eight MiGs from 177th IAP, headed by 1st Squadron leader Capt Mikhailov, that had taken off from Antung to intercept enemy aircraft on the morning of 22 December. The Soviet pilots detected a flight of Sabres near Yomju railway station at 1125 hrs, and Nikolay Vorobyov later recalled;

'I was the first to see the F-86s flying in a diamond formation at an altitude of 12,000 m (39,000 ft). I went after them, climbing, while the rest of our group dropped behind. I levelled off behind the trailing Sabre at an altitude of about 12,200-12,400 m and closed in from its starboard side to a range of 100 m. I fired a burst, but it passed about 1-1.5 m too high and to the left of its wing. The second passed slightly below, while the Sabre started banking to starboard. I followed him, but the third burst went to the right of the F-86. I did not have to aim again as the fourth burst hit the Sabre, which actually flew into it. One 37 mm cannon round hit its tailpipe. Debris and wreckage flew at me. The range could not have been more than 80 m (90 yrd) at that moment. The Sabre caught fire and dived. The pilot did not bail out. He must have been killed.

'Watching the Sabre going down in flames, I shouted "One down! Falling down! On fire!" When I released the transmitter button I heard a voice from the command-and-control post telling me to "Stop yelling! We can see it". The remaining three Sabres broke off by diving. After the camera gun film had been developed, flight instructor Safronov, who had arrived from Moscow, told me at the debriefing "I've never seen pictures with such close-ups of enemy aircraft".'

Vorobyov's victim was Capt Bach, who managed to eject from his F-86A (49-1176) and was taken prisoner soon after he landed in North Korean territory. The stricken Sabre crashed 40-45 km (25-28 miles) southeast of Sinuiju.

Another pilot from Mikhailov's group had chased the three remaining F-86s, and he too was credited with a kill, although he did not report that his victim had crashed (and no other Sabres were lost during this action).

Later that same day MiGs and Sabres clashed yet again when eight Anshan-based aircraft from 177th IAP's 2nd Squadron engaged 16 Sabres. Soviet pilots were credited with three kills (no losses were recorded by the USAF), but two MiGs did not return – one pilot successfully ejected, but flight leader Snr Lt Barsegyan was killed. A third MiG made it back to base with six shell holes in its fuselage. Proving that exaggerated claims were not unique to the communist pilots, the 4th FW was credited with six MiG-15 kills on 22 December!

Forty-eight hours later Capt Stepan Naumenko scored two more kills in two separate dogfights with the Sabres (no losses were recorded by the 4th FW), and in so doing became the first Soviet pilot to score five victories in Korea. Naumenko was immediately made a HSU for his successes.

By the end of the month, 50th IAD pilots had claimed six Sabres, two Thunderjets and two Shooting Stars destroyed between 17 and 31 December in several aerial engagements. F-86 pilots had been credited with the destruction of seven MiG-15s during the same period.

JANUARY – JUNE 1951

Following the frenzied aerial engagements of late December, a relative calm set in after the New Year. Indeed, pilots of 50th IAD did not encounter any enemy aircraft in early January apart from a solitary B-29 intercepted by pilots from 177th IAP on the 10th. The lull ended ten days later when USAF fighter-bombers stepped up their attacks on North Korean transport routes (both road and rail). Formations of 20 to 30 aircraft would make a series of strikes over a 72-hour period between 20 and 23 January, and 50th IAD found itself all but overwhelmed as the division attempted to repel these attacks.

MiG pilots fought for their lives during what they later recalled were the toughest three days of their tour in North Korea. Six dogfights took place, and the division was credited with 15 F-84s and two F-80s destroyed (the USAF admitted the loss of an RF-80A, an F-80C and an F-84E, all on 21 January). F-84E pilots in turn claimed four MiG-15s.

The aerial battles of the 23rd proved to be the last for 29th GvIAP, as its tour of duty ended the following day when 27 of its MiGs were flown north to Anshan. Groundcrews followed the fighters two days later. On 3-5 February, these MiGs-15bis were handed over to 72nd GvIAP, 151st GvIAD, which was preparing for its second Korean War tour.

Pilots of 177th IAP remained in the frontline for a further two weeks after 29th GvIAP had pulled out, and during this time its pilots claimed four F-80s and an F-84 in several engagements. Finally, on 6 February, 177th IAP flew its last combat sortie over North Korea. The regiment then passed its MiGs onto 151st GvIAD too, which replaced 50th IAD at Antung, before joining 29th GvIAP at Anshan. The two units subsequently departed for the Soviet Union a few days later.

Pilots of 151st GvIAD resumed operations in early February, with 28th GvIAP flying from Antung and 72nd GvIAP staying at Anshan to continue the conversion training of Chinese pilots destined to fly the MiG-15. Following their sustained efforts in late January, USAF fighter-bombers were relatively inactive over the Yalu River throughout February, although 28th GvIAP had several encounters with F-80s and B-29s between 9 February and 1 March. These clashes resulted in MiG pilots being credited with 13 victories for the loss of a single MiG-15bis, which was lost while dogfighting with F-80s on 1 March. The USAF, however, gave credit for this victory to a B-29 gunner from the 98th BG.

Two B-29 kills were attributed to 28th GvIAP CO, and future ace, Lt Col V I Kolyadin on 14 February (no losses recorded by USAF) and 1 March (three losses confirmed).

On 2 March the 2nd Squadron of 72nd GvIAP, led by Maj Bordun, redeployed to Antung, and three days later the US Army's Corps of Engineers completed repairs to Suwon airfield, thus enabling the

Deputy CO of the 28th GvIAP, Lt Col Boris Mukhin (who scored 12 individual and three group victories during World War 2, plus one in Korea) and flight leader Sergey Korobov (16 World War 2 victories, plus one in Korea) pose in their civilian attire during a spell of leave in China in 1951

F-86-equipped 334th Fighter Squadron (FS) of the 4th FW to operate from there. Sabres could now reach the Yalu River, and the first dogfight of 1951 between the premier USAF fighter and MiG-15s took place on 6 March – the result, however, was inconclusive.

On the 12th, 151st GvIAD endured its busiest day of combat in 1951 when the division's pilots flew 56 sorties and fought in two large-scale dogfights. They claimed three aircraft destroyed (no losses were recorded by UN forces), but lost two MiGs and their pilots in return.

Based on debriefing reports and camera gun film shot during the course of the day, Kolyadin was credited with downing one of three F-86s that the regiment claimed. A second went to the new CO of 72nd GvIAP, Lt Col Boris Mukhin, who added the kill to the 12 individual and three joint victories that he had scored during the Great Patriotic War. The second dogfight on the 12th, fought between ten 28th GvIAP MiGs-15bis and eight F-80Cs, ended in tragedy, however, as two Soviet pilots who were simultaneously attacking the same Shooting Star collided in the heat of the chase. Both aviators were killed and the enemy suffered no loss.

By the end of March 151st GvIAD pilots had scored five aerial victories, with an F-86 credited to Lt Col Kolyadin on the 19th (no loss listed by the 4th FW) giving him his fifth kill of the conflict. Aside from the two MiGs that collided on 12 March, the division had lost two more jet, and their pilots, by month-end. One had crashed into a hill while chasing a Shooting Star on the 17th (the jet's demise was credited to the F-80 pilot by the USAF), while the second was lost during a dogfight with Sabres on the 31st. The USAF had also erroneously credited B-29 gunners with the destruction of two more MiGs on 30 March.

151st GvIAD's 28th and 72nd GvIAPs fought their last battle of the war on 2 April. The following day 324th IAD, headed by I N Kozhedub (the ranking Allied ace of World War 2), was redeployed to Antung. 151st GvIAD was transferred to the second echelon of 64th IAK in Anshan, where its divisional flight crews started training Chinese pilots. They also remained on the alert for potential action, however, with 28th and 72nd GvIAPs being kept ready to reinforce 324th IAD, and 303rd IAD once it arrived in-theatre in early May, should the need arise.

However, apart from individual pilots attached to first echelon air divisions as reinforcements in the summer and autumn of 1951, pilots of 151st GvIAD were not to face the enemy again. The division handed over its MiGs to 435th IAD of the People's Army of Korea in September and then detached from 64th IAK and returned home in October 1951.

324TH IAD

Although new to combat in Korea, 324th IAD (comprising 29th and 176th GvIAP and 196th IAP) had actually been in China since February

1950. Viewed as one of the elite fighter divisions in the Soviet Air Force, 324th IAD had been based at Kubinka, near Moscow, prior to its despatch to the Far East. Its regiments boasted some of the best pilots in the USSR, as they were expected to participate in air displays and also to test new aircraft entering the air force inventory. For instance, 176th GvIAP flight-tested the La-9, 29th GvIAP the MiG-15 and 196th IAP the La-15. This made the regiments the first choice for various overseas tours of duty.

This MiG-15bis sustained damage in a dogfight with a Sabre during early 1951

29th GvIAP left for China in February 1950, while 176th GvIAP and 196th IAP had departed the previous month. In late November 324th IAD and its HQ were brought up to strength and also sent to the Far East. Ivan Kozhedub was appointed divisional commander, the three times HSU having scored 62 victories during 360 combat sorties and 120 aerial engagements in World War 2.

324th IAD personnel arrived at Dongfeng airfield, in Manchuria, in mid-December, and its aircraft followed by rail. They had to be assembled once in-theatre, after which the division's personnel began intensive training to prepare them for combat operations in the Korean Peninsula. 324th IAD remained at Dongfeng until mid-February, when it was transferred to Anshan so as to be closer to the theatre of operations. The division was now assigned to combat duty, but not before being redeployed to Antung on 1-2 April.

Capt Lev Ivanov, flight leader of 196th IAP's 1st Squadron, is seen here in an official portrait taken in April 1951. He went on to score seven Korean War victories

This photograph of Snr Lt Fedor Shebanov of 196th IAP, 324th IAD was also taken in April 1951. He was the first pilot in his regiment to 'make ace' in Korea, a feat he achieved on 22 April 1951. Shebanov had been credited with six kills prior to his death in combat on 26 October 1951. He was the first Soviet MiG ace to lose his life in Korea

324th IAD engaged the enemy for the first time just 24 hours after arriving at its new base, but this action proved to be anything but a success. Although a pilot from 176th GvIAP was credited with downing an F-86 (the 4th FW lost a Sabre, although it claimed this was due to fuel exhaustion), a MiG-15 was shot down and its pilot killed. Two more MiGs managed to limp home with serious battle damage, and they were later considered to be fit only for scrapping. The end result of this clash was a clear victory for USAF Sabres, with the 4th FW claiming three kills.

The division's pilots were more successful on 4 April, when Capt Lev Ivanov (196th IAP 1st Squadron flight leader) scored the first of his seven Korean War victories during an early morning engagement. He reported;

'We were scrambled to intercept an RB-45C reconnaissance aircraft, escorted by four F-86s. We closed in on a head-on course and engaged in a dogfight. We had been in the air for quite some time, and had already dropped our external fuel tanks. We made a couple of attack runs and broke off. I was credited with an F-86 kill. I got behind it and hit its tail.

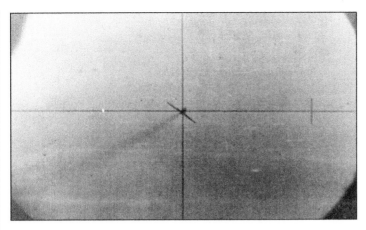

A frame from the camera gun film exposed by Snr Lt Shebanov of the 196th IAP, 324th IAD on 4 April 1951. He fired two medium-length bursts from all three cannon at this F-86 from 250 m (270 yrd) during the course of the engagement

Yet another future ace photographed in April 1951, Capt Ivan Suchkov of the 176th GvIAP, 324th IAD was credited with ten Korean War victories

The jet started billowing smoke and falling out of the sky. The kill was confirmed by ground observers.'

No such loss was recorded by the 4th FW, however.

Snr Lt Fedor Shebanov of the same regiment distinguished himself later that same day whilst flying one of eight MiG-15s scrambled by the 3rd Squadron of 196th IAP to intercept enemy fighters – Shebanov was the leader of the second flight. The MiGs failed to find the USAF jets, however, so squadron leader Capt Nikolay Shelamonov (who would claim five kills) was ordered by his controller to sweep through the area at top speed instead.

Having still failed to find the enemy, the flight turned for home. As he neared Antung, Shelamonov then made the mistake of slowing down to 850 kmh (530 mph) before commencing his descent, rather than losing speed closer to home. A pair of Sabres attempted to capitalise on this error by making a high-speed attack on the MiGs, but they overshot their targets. Focused more on landing than combat, all the Soviet pilots, with the exception of Shebanov, failed to notice that they were under attack.

Reacting quickly, but neglecting to warn his squadronmates of the enemy's presence, Shebanov went after the trailing F-86, opening fire from a range of 250 m (270 yrd). With its greater speed, the Sabre eventually outran the MiG, but not before Shebanov had managed to fire seven 37 mm and 28 23 mm rounds at it – some of these shells hit their target and the Sabre started smoking. It climbed, turned to port and headed for Anju. Although US sources state that no Sabres were lost that day, 324th IAD records state that 'The F-86 downed by Snr Lt Shebanov was found by Maj Zhuchenko near Anju on 5 April 1951'. This victory was the first of six kills credited to Fedor Shebanov during the conflict.

Pilots from 324th IAD encountered B-29s for the first time on 7 April when 16 Superfortresses, escorted by Sabres and Thunderjets, targeted a bridge over the Yalu River. The ensuing engagement resulted in the loss of a 196th IAP MiG-15, although its pilot, Snr Lt Andrushko, ejected safely (no kill claims were made by USAF pilots). Soviet pilots were credited with shooting down two B-29s and an F-84, although only one Superfortress was listed as lost by the Americans. The original divisional combat report stated 'Based on gun camera data and debriefing reports, two B-29s were hit by pilots Subbotin and Suchkov of 176th GvIAP'.

Capt Serafim Subbotin, who already had six World War 2 victories to his credit, would eventually claim nine more kills over Korea. Capt Ivan Suchkov ultimately went one better, scoring ten Korean War victories. Both pilots were credited with downing B-29s on this date for their first kills of the conflict.

The bridge over the Yalu near Sinuiju was the only one left standing by the end of the first week of April following a series of bombing missions by UN aircraft. Yet despite these attacks, the flow of freight and troops passing over the bridge did not slacken. Four-dozen B-29s from the 9th,

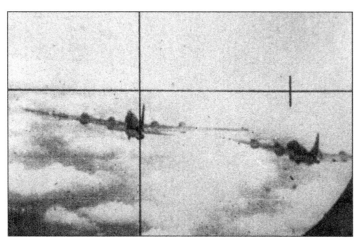

This still taken from Capt Ivan Suchkov's gun camera film clearly shows him targeting a 307th BW B-29 on 7 April 1951. He was credited with the destruction of a Superfortress on this date

98th and 307th BGs targeted it again on 12 April, the bombers being escorted by 39 F-84Es from the 27th Fighter Escort Group (FEG). Sabres from the 4th FW provided high-altitude cover.

When the B-29s were detected, 324th IAD had a squadron of eight MiG-15s on standby status No 1 and two squadrons on standby status Nos 2 and 3, with a fourth unit having its jets refuelled following their recent return from a mission. 324th IAD CO Ivan Kozhedub described what happened next;

'When the first enemy group was detected I put my subordinate units, which had been on alert status Nos 2 and 3, on high alert. When it became clear that the enemy was heading our way, I decided to scramble two groups of fighters (numbering eight and six jets), headed by Capts Shelamonov and Tkatskiy, from 196th IAP. They took off at 0955 hrs.

'At 1000 hrs I ordered two more groups of eight and six MiG-15s from 176th GvIAP, led by Capts Konstantin Sheberstov (who eventually achieved 12 Korean War victories) and Murashev, to repulse the second group of enemy bombers. When our fighters took off and climbed, they were guided to the bombers by a ground-based command and control post. At 1010 hrs our fighter pilots reported seeing a formation of B-29s.'

196th IAP flight leader Capt Lev Ivanov was the first to spot the bombers, and moments later fired a burst at the leading B-29s. The MiG pilot then focused his attention on a solitary bomber, firing at it from a range of 600-700 m (650-750 yrd). His two short bursts passed under the target, however, so he closed to within 300-400 m (325-430 yrd) and fired two more bursts. These slammed into the B-29's fuselage and forced the now smoking bomber out of formation. Ivanov's wingman, Snr Lt Kochegarov (who was to score three victories in the conflict), attacked another Superfortress and set its wing tanks alight. This B-29 also started descending towards the sea, with smoke billowing from its wing.

MiG-15 111025 was flown by Snr Lt Gogolev (two Korean War victories) of the 2nd Squadron, 176th GvIAP, 324th IAD from Antung in April 1951

A mass of aircraft, interspersed with cannon and machine gun fire, flames and smoke, slugged it out over the Yalu for almost 40 minutes, Capt Tkatskiy's group of six jets fighting B-29s, F-80s and F-86s.

Although the Superfortresses were the primary targets, several MiG pilots, like Snr Lt Fukin (another to score three Korean War kills), had their hands full engaging the bomber escorts. He managed to get behind one of the Shooting Stars and fired three accurate bursts from 150-200 m (160-220 yrd) that hit the F-80's fuselage. Its starboard landing gear dropped down and the fighter plunged earthward – although the USAF admitted the loss of four B-29s on the 12th, no F-80s were reportedly destroyed.

While Capt Tkatskiy's flight was busy fighting its way through to the Superfortresses, Capt Shelamonov's eight MiG-15s were heading for the Cholsan area to intercept enemy fighters detected at an altitude of 11,000 m (36,000 ft). Finding nothing upon their arrival in the target area, the pilots were ordered to attack a nearby formation of bombers instead. Once they had descended down to the B-29s' height, the Soviet pilots quickly spotted two groups of Superfortresses flying in tight formation. The MiGs overhauled the first group of B-29s and made three passes at them, while simultaneously repulsing the escorting Shooting Stars. Soviet documents state that the escorting fighters were F-80s, and this is confirmed by gun camera film, yet US historians persist in stating that 27th FEG F-84s and 4th FW Sabres were the only fighters present.

The MiGs, led by Capt Sheberstov, engaged the first aircraft in the second group of Superfortresses some 30-35 km (19-22 miles) southeast of Antung at 1018 hrs. Two B-29s attacked by Sheberstov and Subbotin were downed and another was seriously damaged. The combat formation was broken up by this attack and the bombers dropped their ordnance before reaching the target. Capts Grigoriy Ges (who had five World War 2 kills to his name, and who would score eight more over Korea) and Ivan Suchkov and Snr Lt Petr Milaushkin (11 Korean War victories) claimed three more B-29s destroyed in follow-up attacks.

The squadron headed by Capt Murashev (one Korean War victory), which followed Sheberstov's group into the fray, split up into pairs and attacked the first Superfortress group's trailing formation 30 km (19 miles) southeast of Antung. Snr Lt Plitkin (four Korean War victories) singled out the leading B-29 in this formation, and he saw the bomber burst into flames, bank to port and drop away after two long bursts fired from a distance of 300-600 m (320-650 yrd). He also reported seeing its crew bail out. Plitkin's wingman, Snr Lt Obraztsov, downed a second B-29.

Four more MiGs had been scrambled at 1013 hrs to reinforce the Soviet fighter groups already committed to the battle, the newcomers being led by squadron leader and HSU Capt Aleksander Vasko. A pilot with vast experience, he had flown 400 combat sorties in World War 2, fought in 100 air battles and shot down 18 enemy aircraft, to which he would add three Korean War victories. Vasko's four MiGs duly encountered eight B-29s, escorted by fighters, 15 km (nine miles) southeast of Antung. He and his wingman attacked the bombers, while the second pair in his group, led by Capt Sergey Kramarenko (one kill in World War 2 and 13 over Korea), engaged the enemy fighters. Kramarenko was subsequently credited with downing an F-84, although the USAF recorded no losses.

Eight more MiG-15s from 196th IAP, which represented the final divisional reserves, were sent into action at 1023 hrs. They were headed by the 2nd Squadron's Snr Lt Boris Bokach, a pilot who had flown 80 World War 2 combat sorties, participated in seven aerial engagements and shot down two enemy aircraft, with six more to follow over Korea.

His group had just reached operating altitude when they encountered four B-29s and two groups of eight fighters 15 km south of the bridge.

Capt Nikolay Shelamonov, who was 196th IAP's 3rd Squadron leader, scored five Korean War victories

Continuing to climb, they initially attacked the USAF fighters head-on, before turning to line up behind the bombers. As they did so, the Soviet pilots were engaged by two groups of eight F-80s and F-86s. Bokach immediately ordered Snr Lt Boris Abakumov's flight to keep the US fighters occupied while he led his own flight in against the B-29s.

All four pilots in the squadron leader's flight opened fire simultaneously as they closed on the Superfortresses, damaging three of the bombers. Capt Nazarkin (three Korean War victories), who was leading the second pair of MiG-15s, singled out one of the damaged B-29s and knocked out both of the engines on its starboard wing. With these trailing flames, he exhausted the rest of his ammunition on its cockpit from a range of just 100-150 m. Nazarkin reported that the bomber then banked to starboard and fell away in a blazing inferno.

Meanwhile, Abakumov (who would score five Korean War victories) had fought off the fighters and led his flight after a group of Superfortresses heading for the bridge. He fired at the leader and then attacked its wingman. Having exhausted his ammunition, Abakumov headed for home, thus bringing to an end one of the largest, and longest, aerial engagements of the Korean War.

So, what were the results of this huge battle? Documents from 324th IAD state;

'The first group of enemy bombers suffered heavy losses inflicted by our fighters and was forced to drop its bombs before reaching the target. The second group, also attacked by our fighters, sustained heavy losses and bombed the southern outskirts of the city of Sinuiju. The third enemy bomber group, which encountered insufficient resistance from our fighters, managed to bomb the railway bridge. We had used most of our assets in repulsing the first two air strikes by the time the third group made its appearance. Flight crews conducted their part in the air engagements competently, capitalising on the disadvantages of enemy aircraft.

'A total of 40 MiG-15s, 52-60 B-29s and 60-75 enemy fighters participated in the engagement. Soviet pilots downed up to 11 B-29s and two F-80s and damaged 14 B-29s and five fighters, suffering no losses in return – only five Soviet aircraft sustained two to seven shell-holes.'

On 15 April 324th IAD commander Ivan Kozhedub wrote in his combat summary that the North Korean authorities had reported capturing three B-29 flight crews. In addition, a crew had bailed out over Sinmi-do Island at 1100 hrs and their aircraft had crashed into the sea. Sonchon's chief of police confirmed this. Soviet pilots were eventually credited with downing ten B-29s and four enemy fighters.

These scores contrast sharply with USAF losses and victory claims. As previously mentioned, according to American records, three B-29s were lost during the clash, and a fourth was damaged beyond repair and scrapped after returning to base. No fighters were lost. The USAF credited B-29 gunners with the destruction of seven MiGs, and four more were claimed by F-86 pilots.

The loss of so many B-29s proved to the USAF that the heavy bomber could no longer be employed in the MiG-15's area of operations during daylight hours. Morale among Superfortress squadrons had been undermined, and flightcrews dreaded making further attacks on Sinuiju.

Like many of his contemporaries in 196th IAP, Capt Boris Bokach was a veteran of fighter combat in World War 2. The regiment's 2nd Squadron leader, he scored six Korean War victories to add to his two successes from 1944-45

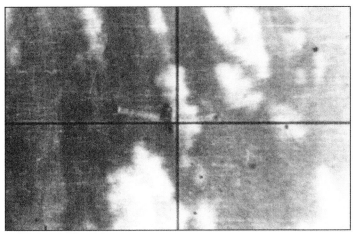

Future nine-kill ace Capt Serafim Subbotin of 176th GvIAP, 324th IAD targets a USAF F-84 Thunderjet that was attempting to protect B-29s during the huge aerial battle that took place on 12 April 1951. The Thunderjet succeeded in getting away, as no F-84s were downed on this date

MiG-15 108023 from 324th IAD was damaged in a dogfight during April 1951. The aircraft has had its wings and horizontal tailplane removed so as to allow them to be repaired

Shortly after the 12 April mission, USAF Far East Air Force (FEAF) headquarters received a report from Bomber Command stating that a total of 25 B-29s – one in four of the available Superfortresses – had been damaged during attacks on the Yalu bridges. Such figures far exceeded the ten per cent loss rate that was considered to be the upper limit of what was acceptable. FEAF commander, Lt Gen George Stratemeyer, banned further B-29 sorties to the Sinuiju area until an effective way of escorting them could be found. As it transpired, no further B-29 raids were mounted on the bridges near Sinuiju.

Fighters from 324th IAD fought four more air engagements before the month of April came to an end. Snr Lt Fedor Shebanov of 196th IAP scored his fifth Korean War victory on 22 April, thus making him the third MiG-15 ace of the conflict. His success was one of 34 enemy aircraft (one RB-45C, 12 B-29s, one B-26, 13 F-86s, two F-84s and five F-80s) credited to the division as shot down during April. Soviet losses amounted to eight MiG-15s and two pilots killed in action.

All of these aircraft were downed by Sabres, which, for the RD-45F-powered MiG-15, had proven to be a tough nut to crack – the USAF had credited F-86 pilots and B-29 gunners with 22 MiG victories.

In mid-April Kozhedub's division exchanged its combat-weary MiG-15s with 151st GvIAD, receiving 47 MiG-15bis fighters in return. The latter had been operated by the 50th IAD and 151st GvIAD in-theatre since December 1950. In late May 1951 324th IAD received an additional 16 MiGs-15bis fresh from the Novosibirsk Aircraft Factory.

NEW DIVISION ENTERS COMBAT

With UN aerial activity clearly on the increase as the weather improved over Korea, 303rd IAD was sent into action in early May alongside 324th IAD. Like the latter division, 303rd IAD (and its trio of regiments – 18th GvIAP and 177th and 523rd IAPs) had been protecting Moscow prior to

being redeployed to Primorie, in eastern USSR, in July 1950. 177th IAP was subsequently sent to Liaodong Peninsula, in China, two months later. 17th IAP from neighbouring 190th IAD (which was itself later committed to the Korean War) was duly attached to 303rd IAD on 4 October to replace 177th IAP.

Pilots from 303rd IAD were placed on combat alert during the second week of October, and they were called to arms on 26 December. On that date, 523rd IAP pilots Capt Stepan Bakhaev (who had flown 112 combat sorties during World War 2, fighting in 28 air battles and scoring 11 individual and two group victories, to which he would add 11 more kills over Korea) and Snr Lt Kotov intercepted and shot down an RB-29 reconnaissance aircraft near Cape Xiexiu.

On 23 January 1951, 303rd IAD was attached to 64th IAK. Three months later, divisional regiments transferred to northern and eastern Chinese airfields near Mukden and were instructed to ready themselves for combat duty. 18th GvIAP was redeployed to Antung on 8 May, and its pilots flew their first combat sorties that same day. 17th and 523rd IAPs stayed behind in Mukden, however, where they continued their programme of intensive combat training.

Following the large-scale battles of April 1951, May turned out to be a fairly quiet time for 64th IAK, with Soviet pilots engaging the enemy on the 1st, 9th and 20th only. The MiG units were credited with shooting down seven enemy aircraft (four Sabres and three Thunderjets), although USAF records reveal no losses on these dates. Two MiGs-15bis were downed in dogfights with F-86s, but their pilots ejected safely, and a third fighter sustained ten shell holes – the USAF credited the 4th FW with five kills and a B-29 gunner with a solitary victory during May.

Another forward airfield was completed in Tatung-kao in late May, and 303rd IAD's 523rd IAP redeployed there on 28 May.

June proved to be a considerably busier month for the MiG-15 units, and on the 1st 303rd IAD opened its Korean War combat score and also suffered its first loss.

That day, fighters from 324th and 303rd IADs (including ten MiG-15bis from 18th GvIAP) were led into combat against B-29s by squadron leader Capt P N Antonov – he would claim seven Korean War victories by the end of his tour. Having fought his way past eight escorting Sabres, Snr Lt Evgeniy Stelmakh single-handedly attacked four B-29s and managed to shoot one of them down. He then used up the rest of his ammunition inflicting considerable damage on two more enemy aircraft, after which he was set upon by the Sabre escorts. Stelmakh's controls were soon knocked out and he was forced to eject.

Chinese infantrymen mistook the Soviet pilot for an American when he reached the ground and duly tried to take him prisoner. Stelmakh in turn took them for disguised American saboteurs and started shooting at them with his pistol. He managed to hit three Chinese soldiers in the ensuing gunfight, but saved the last bullet for himself.

While Stelmakh was fighting for his life, his comrades from 18th GvIAP had intercepted a formation of F-51Ds from the 18th FBG that had been searching for survivors from the B-29 that he had just downed. In the ensuing dogfight, two Mustangs were claimed to have been shot down – one as an individual kill and the second as a group victory (the

Photographed in May 1951, Snr Lt Vladimir Alfeev of 196th IAP scored seven Korean War victories

USAF lost a solitary F-51D to MiGs on this date). Snr Lt Lev Shchukin was credited with the individual victory, this being the first of 15 kills that would subsequently make him 18th GvIAP's ranking ace. B-29 gunners and F-86 pilots claimed two kills apiece on 1 June.

The second half of June saw 64th IAK routinely clashing with USAF fighter units, the corps' five MiG regiments within 303rd and 324th IADs having by then been concentrated around Antung. This included 17th IAP, which redeployed to Tatung-kao on 11 June.

Capt Sergey Kramarenko, who eventually became 176th GvIAP's leading ace with 13 kills, fought one of his most intense air battles on 17 June;

'Our group of four took off to intercept 12 enemy aircraft. We detected them immediately. I turned sharply and launched an attack, closing in on an enemy flight and then opening fire. Suddenly, I felt something amiss. I looked back and saw a Sabre just 80 m behind me. I had the impression that he was already firing at me, as I saw flashes coming from the nose of his aircraft.

'I was at an altitude of about 8000 m (26,000 ft) and decided on a wingover. I pushed the control stick and rudder pedal sharply. My fighter went into a dive. I looked back and saw three Sabres, which I hadn't noticed before as they were attacking me from above. The Sabres were heavier and started catching me in a dive. I was thinking that I had to do something when I saw clouds below. I recovered from the dive at an altitude of about 5000-6000 m (16,000-19,500 ft), flew right into the cloud and made a 90-degree turn.

'I cut through the cloud, climbed and made a turn to starboard to get to the American aircraft. I saw the three Sabres below, searching for me. I decided to attack. They noticed me and split. Two of them headed left and down, while the third started climbing to the right. I thought that if I started down after the two enemy aircraft, the one to starboard would shoot me down immediately, but if I went for the latter the remaining pair would chase me. I decided to attack the singleton.

'Due to my superior height, I closed in quickly and opened fire. The Sabre immediately burst into flames, half-rolled and then started falling. I followed him to see what would happen, but then I remembered I had two more Sabres to deal with! I looked back and saw them on my tail. I made a climbing turn and saw they were catching me. Then I made a wingover, dived, plunged into cloud and tried to deceive the Americans. In the cloud I made a turn to starboard.

'The Sabre pilots were clearly combat veterans, as they didn't follow me, but stayed above, waiting for me to come out of the cloud. When I did, they dropped behind me again. I then had to fight them two-to-one. I could have tried to break off by climbing, but the range was too low and they would have been able to shoot me down if I'd flown a straight course. So I tried to manoeuvre my way out with slanting loops and wingovers. The Americans turned out to be seasoned pilots. My aircraft and I experienced high G-loads – the blood rushed from my head and everything went dark. My opponents were in a better position as they were wearing anti-G suits. I manoeuvred so as to edge towards the Yalu.

'After 15 minutes of high-G manoeuvring I was almost exhausted. I thought that if I couldn't break off, the Americans would eventually get me.

I decided to head for the bridge over the Yalu River, which was protected by our air defence artillery. When carrying out yet another manoeuvre, I levelled off instead of climbing and accelerated up to 1030 kmh (645 mph) by descending slightly. I looked back and saw the Americans lagging slightly behind, as they hadn't expected me to climb. They were about 800-1000 m (860-1100 yrd) behind me when my jet started to roll. I had to extend the air brakes, level off, retract the air brakes and accelerate again. That was what I did again and again – accelerate into a climb of 50-60 degrees, brake, level off and accelerate again.

'Naturally, the enemy fighters gradually caught up with me when the range was down to about 600 m (650 yrd). Air defence artillery then opened up, and shells started exploding ahead. But if I'd turned away from the bridge the Sabres would have had me. There was no way out. I headed right into the shell bursts. The aircraft shook and was thrown from side to side as if it were taxiing on cobblestones. I gripped the control column tightly and sat there more dead than alive. I got out of the flak "cloud" after about 15-20 seconds. It was sunny and calm. I saw the Americans retreating – they didn't dare follow me, and they turned towards the sea.'

NEW ACE

On 18 June 324th IAD added a second ace to its ranks, and the fourth for 64th IAK in Korea, when Capt Serafim Subbotin of 176th GvIAP scored his fifth and sixth victories in unusual circumstances. A group of eight MiGs from his regiment had scrambled to intercept 16 F-86s, and during one attack Capt Subbotin closed to within 100 m of a Sabre and opened fire. His rounds hit the jet's fuselage and cockpit and the USAF fighter then went into a dive and exploded in mid-air. At that very moment two more Sabres approached Subbotin's MiG from behind. Trying to evade them, the Soviet pilot came across a second MiG-15 being attacked by another pair of F-86s.

Subbotin opened fire, but seconds later his fighter shuddered as machine gun rounds struck his engine, causing it to flame out. Kerosene then started flowing into the cockpit, and billowing thick white smoke obscured the pilot's view. Subbotin jettisoned his canopy and, as the smoke was being drawn out, he looked back to see a pair of Sabres closing in for the kill. The MiG pilot was unable to shake them off his tail, despite performing a series of sharp banks in his engineless fighter, and the Sabres closed to within 50 m of him. Serafim Subbotin later recalled;

'I went into a starboard spin. When recovering, I was attacked twice by the Sabres, which were close behind. They were firing their weapons all the time. The last burst damaged my aileron controls, and the insolent enemy kept chasing me and firing at point-blank range. I extended the air brakes and almost immediately felt something hit the rear of my MiG – the impact was accompanied by a horrible grinding noise. A second later I saw an F-86 with a torn-off starboard wing panel on my portside. The Sabre had crashed into me. My damaged MiG started darting from side to side, creating various G-loads. I was thrown about inside the cockpit. When negative G lifted me out of my seat, I bailed out of the now uncontrollable aircraft. I landed in mountains about 12 km (7.5 miles) away from the town of Taisen.'

The 4th FW admitted the loss of a solitary F-86A on 18 June, thus confirming at least one of Subbotin's kills.

The action continued the following day when 17th IAP pilot Snr Lt Nikolay Sutyagin, who would eventually become the ranking ace of the Korean War with 22 victories, opened his account. Ten MiGs from the unit, headed by regimental CO Maj Grigoriy Pulov (who scored eight kills in Korea), took off to intercept enemy aircraft.

While the Soviet fighters were flying through cloud, a pair of Sabres attempted to attack them. Sutyagin spotted the F-86s, however, and he ordered his wingman, Vasiliy Shulev (seven Korean War victories), to follow him as he engaged the enemy fighters in a vertical dogfight. Sutyagin managed to drop behind the trailing Sabre and open fire, although his first burst passed ahead of the jet and the second fell behind it. The American pilots immediately nosed over into a steep dive after pulling out of a loop and ran for Korea Bay, with the MiGs in hot pursuit.

Moments later Sutyagin fired a long burst at the F-86 wingman from 100 m, and this time his rounds found the target. The Sabre caught fire and went into a vertical dive, before ultimately crashing into a hill and exploding.

At that very moment Snr Lt Shulev was diving after the leading Sabre, firing at it from a distance of 300-400 m. The MiG accelerated to such a high speed as it headed earthward that its sliding canopy tore off at an altitude of 2000 m (6500 ft). Shulev hastily aborted the chase and lost the still diving enemy aircraft as they raced across North Korea at low-level. Again, the 4th FW noted the loss of a Sabre in combat with MiG-15s.

Capt Grigoriy Ges of 176th GvIAP took his Korean War tally to five victories on 20 June when he downed a Mustang. Closing to within 100 m of the 35th FG fighter-bomber, his cannon and machine gun rounds tore the F-51 apart. As the American fighter literally disintegrated, its port wing hit the MiG's tail unit and destroyed its stabiliser, pulling Ges' aircraft down in the process. With its rudder jammed, the Soviet fighter could not descend or climb, although Ges did manage to bank the fighter over. This was fortuitous, as moments after destroying the F-51, the newly crowned ace and his wingman were attacked by four F-86s.

The Sabre pilots hit Ges' wingman, Snr Lt Nikolaev (although they claimed no MiG-15 kills on this date – the USAF officially lost a solitary F-51D), but Ges himself managed to evade the attack, despite being at the controls of a crippled aircraft. Joining up with Nikolaev, he did his best to cover his wounded comrade-in-arms as they limped back to base. On reaching the airfield, Ges ordered Nikolaev to land, while he climbed up to altitude in order to study the behaviour of his aircraft at low speeds with landing flaps extended. Satisfied that he could get the MiG down in one piece, Ges put the fighter into a shallow dive and successfully landed his heavily damaged fighter.

Intensive combat operations continued through to the end of June 1951, with 64th IAK pilots being credited with the destruction of 52 enemy aircraft (two B-29s, an F-94, 27 F-86s, 13 F-80s and nine F-51s) during the course of the month. Many future aces had opened their combat scores during this period, but eight MiG-15bis had in turn been shot down and four Soviet pilots killed in action. USAF F-86 pilots and B-29 gunners claimed 14 MiG victories during June 1951.

JULY – DECEMBER 1951

Following the near-daily clashes between MiG-15s and USAF aircraft between 15 and 30 June 1951, July and August saw less action due to the onset of cloudy weather over North Korea and northeastern China. The cloud base frequently started at an altitude of just 600-700 m (2000-2300 ft) and topped out at 10,000 m (32,500 ft). Rain also fell with a monotonous frequency, and the mornings were often foggy. Such weather did little to encourage high-speed aerial warfare, but the Soviet pilots sometimes had little choice but to take off and fight when UN aircraft were detected over North Korea.

196th IAP pilots were scrambled to intercept a group of American aircraft in wet and murky conditions on 21 July 1951. Included in their number was future 19-kill ace Lt Col E G Pepelyaev, who recalled;

'Once I downed an F-94 in a turn by shooting its tail unit off. Enemy aircraft made their sorties in the daytime. It was foggy, and our airfield was totally misted over. Enemy aircraft had almost reached Mukden, and corps commanding officer Col Belov was reluctant to let us intercept them – he initially forbade us from taking off due to the poor weather conditions. I was on alert, and by the time we were cleared to take off the enemy group had passed our airfield and was on its way back home.

'We caught up with eight F-94s when they were already approaching the coast. In fact I was no longer allowed to attack them, as they were already above the Yellow Sea. I radioed Capt Bokach and told him to go for the leading four aircraft, while I targeted the rear flight myself. I attacked while still climbing. I engaged one of the F-94s from below and saw debris flying around, but I didn't follow it any longer. I levelled off and saw another F-94 making a turn to port. I shot its tail unit off while it was still turning and the wreckage flew towards me. I even ducked my head, but the debris missed my aircraft.

'The F-94s then broke formation and scattered. My pilots followed, each attacking their own targets. We were already over the Yellow Sea, so I ordered the battle to be aborted. Everything could have been different if I'd been allowed to take off half-an-hour earlier.

'I didn't know the exact results of the engagement. Our regiment was credited with seven or eight victories. I even had to credit one of my pilots with downing two F-94s, which had apparently collided in mid-air during his attack. I didn't believe it, but the divisional command ordered me to confirm that this had indeed happened.'

In fact, the aircraft engaged by the Soviet pilots were F9F Panthers from US Marine Corps fighter unit VMF-311, based in South Korea, rather than F-94 Starfire nightfighters. US sources state that F9Fs had clashed with MiG-15s in the day's only air battle, and Pepelyaev's camera gun film confirms that his adversary was indeed a Panther. According to

Lt Col Evgeniy Pepelyaev, CO of 196th IAP, 324th IAD, was the second-ranking Soviet fighter ace of the Korean War with 19 kills. He is pictured here at Antung during the summer of 1951

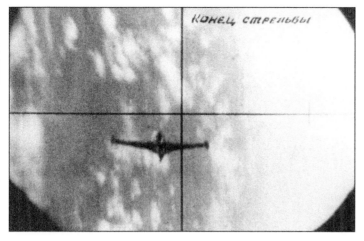

КОНЕЦ СТРЕЛЬБЫ

US Marine Corps F9F-2B BuNo
123464 of VMF-311 is framed in
the cross-hairs of Lt Col Pepelyaev's
gunsight at a range of just 200 m on
21 July 1951. The Panther was shot
down by the Soviet ace moments
later, Pepelyaev erroneously
claiming that he had destroyed
an F-94 Starfire

the Marine Corps, only a single F9F
was lost to the MiGs on this date.

196th IAP's CO stated in his
combat report of 21 July;

'Pilots who took part in the
air engagement reported downing
seven F-94s, while interpreted gun
camera films show four F-94s
shot down. Based on information
received from the North Korean
police, local people and North
Korean and Chinese army units, it
was determined that the vertical tail
and rudder of an F-94 downed in
the engagement were found near
Pakchon. The Zonnon police saw an aircraft with a torn off wing falling
in the Chonju area. The search is still in progress. The crash sites of the
other enemy aircraft shot down have yet to be detected.'

Soviet pilots were credited with downing a total of 24 enemy aircraft in
July, including seven 'F-94s' (F9Fs), 13 F-86s, an F-84 and an F-89. Maj
Nikolay Sutyagin of 17th IAP and Capt Sergey Kramarenko of 176th
GvIAP were amongst those to claim kills, thus taking their tallies to five –
many more were to follow for both pilots. 64th IAK lost four MiGs and
three pilots during July, although the USAF credited its F-86 and B-29
units with nine MiG-15s destroyed.

August proved to be a less successful month for the MiG pilots,
however, due to the onset of more bad weather. Combat sorties were
performed exclusively by 303rd IAD, with 324th IAD being allowed a
short break from operations. The corps command used this lull in the
fighting to give pilots a rest, review the results they had achieved and
summarise the overall combat experience.

A conference on flight tactics, which involved pilots from both
divisions, was also held at Tatung-kao airfield on 23-28 August. The
results of combat operations by Soviet pilots between 1 November 1950
and 1 August 1951 were listed as follows – 6667 combat sorties flown,
187 group air engagements fought and 231 enemy aircraft shot down for
the loss of 37 MiGs and 21 pilots. In August Soviet pilots scored 14 more
victories by downing four Sabres, six Shooting Stars and four Meteors,
losing six MiG-15bis fighters and a pilot in the process. USAF pilots (all
from the 4th FW) made only four victory claims, however.

STALEMATE

By August 1951 the frontline had stabilised on the Hangan River, north
of Seoul, and from now until war's end both sides would launch
offensives and counter-offensives of varying sizes, costing thousands of
lives. Yet despite these bloody campaigns, the frontier between the two
nations on the Korean peninsula would remain the 38th parallel.

The USAF formed the main bulwark against the numerically superior
Korean and Chinese forces, and represented the only means by which
UN forces could cut their supply lines and prevent fresh reinforcements
and supplies from reaching the frontline. As a result, one of the main tasks

facing Soviet pilots was to protect the lines of communications of the Chinese people's army and people's volunteers in the 64th IAK's area of responsibility.

In early September the weather improved considerably, and air engagements were fought once again with a vengeance. In the first ten days of the month the clashes were mainly between MiGs and Sabres, as US fighter pilots tried to keep their Soviet counterparts north of the Yalu River so as to give UN fighter-bombers greater freedom of action.

One such battle was waged on 2 September when MiGs from 17th IAP and 18th GvIAP encountered a large group of Sabres from the 4th FW. Major participants from the Soviet side were Lt Col Aleksander Smorchkov, second-in-command of 18th GvIAP and a man with 282 tactical missions, 36 aerial engagements and four individual kills in World War 2 to his credit (he would claim 12 more victories in Korea), and Maj Dmitriy Oskin, who would score 15 Korean War kills. They sighted a pair of Sabres and immediately went after them, as Smorchkov subsequently recalled;

'Together with Oskin, Dmitriy and Pavlovich, I was flying at 12,000 m (39,000 ft) when we caught two Sabres. They flew in different directions and so did we. I had to follow "my" American almost as far as Pyongyang. First he flipped over and dived, and I followed him. He then began manoeuvring, turning his aircraft right and left, up and down. I tried to get him! I was a little nervous because there was an engagement going on behind me, and the whole American armada was at my back. I thought, "How am I going to get back through them?" I stuck to his tail and followed all his manoeuvres. As I fired at him I thought, "What am I to do? Should I use all my ammunition?" The ground was close and we were now flying over bare mountain peaks. Then, finally, I caught him! The American went up to the left but I didn't follow.

'When he came back down I fired a long burst. Then he flew into it and crashed into the mountaintop. It was the only time that I saw a fighter I had just shot down actually crash. But still I didn't have enough time to see exactly what happened, as I was flying at 1000 kmh (625 mph).

'On my way home I had to pass Korea Bay and then turn west towards the airfield. I'd dropped my external tanks long ago, so there wasn't much fuel left in the main tanks. The Americans were flying towards me from the main battle area. They were watching me, one rather insolent MiG. They began manoeuvring in an attempt to cut me off, but as I was still flying at 1100 kmh (688 mph), I thought I could just push my way through them. Besides, they too must have been short of fuel. I managed to fly through the whole armada and get back home.'

The 4th FW reported the loss of a single F-86 on 2 September, claiming four MiG-15s in return.

Another big battle was fought during the afternoon of 9 September, involving pilots from 17th, 196th and 523rd IAPs and 176th

Lt Col Aleksander Smorchkov, deputy CO of 18th GvIAP, added 12 Korean War victories to the four kills he had scored in World War 2

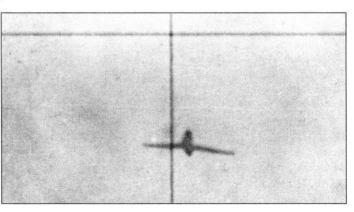

This still was taken from the camera gun film shot by Lt Col Aleksander Smorchkov on 2 September 1951. Framed in the cross-hairs is F-86A 49-1258 from the 4th FW's 335th FS, which the future ace forced to crash into a mountain peak

GvIAP. Future ten-kill ace Snr Lt Dmitriy Samoylov of 523rd IAP scored his first victory during the clash;

'I claimed an F-86 during my first flight as a pair leader. My aircraft was one of six flying in the Anju area, where most aerial engagements usually started because of the river crossings that were often attacked by the Americans. A ground observation post warned us that 24 enemy aircraft were approaching. We saw them coming closer, and Okhay (Capt G U Okhay, who became an ace with 11 kills) led the six of us into a loop. I was on his left, and made a climbing turn to the left. The pair of aircraft on our right made a climbing turn to the right. We then spread out.

Enjoying a cigarette, Snr Lt Dmitriy Samoylov (ten Korean War victories) relaxes with his wingman Snr Lt Mikhail Zykov (four victories) during a break between missions. Both men served with 523rd IAP, 303rd IAD

'Eight Sabres followed us through these manoeuvres and then attacked us from above, thus exploiting their speed advantage. They began shooting at me at from 1000 m (1100 yrd). I cried to my wingman, Mikhail Zykov, "Hold on!" I didn't turn any further and began a spiral climb to port. The Sabres attacked us at a height of 6000-6500 m (19,500-21,000 ft) and pursued us until we had climbed to 11,000 m (35,750 ft). When we were at 10,500 m (34,000 ft), I saw that one group of four Sabres was holding back. When my jet had reached its top speed, I spotted two more F-86s that had followed the previous group into the area. I looked around and saw that the sky was clear, aside from these two jets. I made a half-roll and followed this last pair, which they might not have been expecting me to do. I quickly overtook them and shot down one of the Sabres down.'

No F-86s were lost in action on the 9th according to USAF records, but the 4th FW claimed a solitary MiG-15 kill – B-29 gunners were also credited with downing two Soviet jets.

By September, 64th IAK had started to take a heavy toll of the US fighter-bombers, or at least that is what the official statistics released by the corps stated. Soviet pilots were credited with the destruction of 90 aircraft – 39 F-86s, 28 F-84s, 15 F-80s, two F-51s and six Meteors. As these tallies reveal, 57 per cent of the UN types claimed were attack aircraft. Seven more pilots passed the five-kill mark during the course of the month, thus taking 64th IAK's ace roster to 14. However, the cost of this success had been high, with 303rd and 324th IADs losing five aircraft and two pilots. USAF jets claimed 13 MiGs destroyed, with 12 of these falling to the 4th FW and the final kill being credited to the F-84E-equipped 9th FBS.

As would be the case throughout the war, actual UN casualties were far lower than those given in the documents generated by 64th IAK, but they were still significant nonetheless – at least ten USAF aircraft fell victim to MiGs in September 1951, and a countless number were damaged. Two RAAF Meteor F 8s were also badly shot up, but they made it back to base and were repaired.

September had seen UN fighter-bomber units venturing into the Yalu River area (dubbed 'MiG Alley' by F-86 pilots) in ever-larger numbers, hence the losses suffered by the F-80 and F-84 wings. In light of these reversals, Gen Frank F Everest, commander of the USAF's Fifth Air Force, ordered that there should be no further flights north of the Chongchon River. Fighter-bomber wings were instructed to switch the focus of their operations to the area between the Chongchon River and the North Korea capital of Pyongyang instead. Therefore, in October 1951 this became the main area for action between the MiGs and US fighters and fighter-bombers.

On 6 October, two new aces were created in the form of Maj K Ya Sheberstov of 176th GvIAP and Lt Col E G Pepelyaev of 196th IAP. The latter managed to shoot down an F-86A for his fifth kill, Pepelyaev later recalling that his opponent seemed to be inexperienced. The Soviet pilot had led ten MiGs-15bis aloft at 0851 hrs after 196th IAP had been scrambled when enemy aircraft were spotted heading for Pyongyang. Overflying the Chongchon estuary at an altitude of 8000 m (26,000 ft), 196th IAP pilots found the Sabres and immediately attacked them.

In his first pass, Evgeniy Pepelyaev fired at the F-86 element leader's wingman from 550 m (600 yrd), but was unable to see the results. The Soviet pilot then became the quarry as the second pair of Sabres made a head-on attack. The F-86 leader opened fire on Pepelyaev's aircraft;

'I remember everything as if it was yesterday because this engagement stuck in my mind. I was hit by the F-86 leader, and his rounds tore a big hole in my air intake. I then remembered a pre-war trick. During exercises with other pilots in my unit, I had explored many different ways to shake an adversary off my tail and then gain an advantage over him. I had discovered that the best way of doing this in the nimble MiG-15 was to make a tight climbing turn in one direction, then quickly reverse direction and follow my adversary closely so that when he came out of his climbing turn, I was on his tail.

'On this particular occasion, when dispersing the Sabre flight right and upwards, I flew level, before starting a climbing turn in the formation leader's direction. But as soon as I reached an angle of 40-50 degrees, I switched from flying a right-hand climbing turn to a left-hand one. That put me above, behind and slightly to the right of the Sabre leader. He was now about 100 m (110 yrd) ahead of me, and as I pushed the control column forward in an effort to get him into my gunsight, negative G pulled me out of my seat and spoiled my aim. I quickly flew a half-roll so that I was now being pressed back into my seat.

'As soon as I rolled, the F-86 pilot did the same thing, but by then I had already locked the aiming mark onto his canopy and opened fire from 130 m (140 yrd), slightly to the right. A 37 mm round hit the jet

This fuzzy gun camera still was taken on 6 October 1951 by Lt Col Evgeniy Pepelyaev during a turning fight with F-86A-5 49-1319 of the 4th FW's 336th FS. Having closed to within 130 m of his foe, Pepelyaev opened fire – the white curve just aft of the jet's cockpit shows a 37 mm round impacting the fuselage of the Sabre. The strike left the jet's ejection seat inoperable

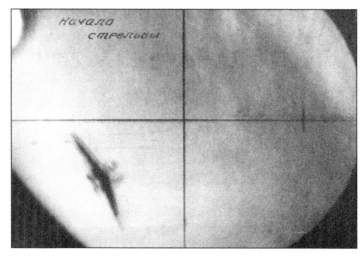

Even fighter pilots as successful as Lt Col Pepelyaev did not always get away scot-free, as this close-up view of his MiG-15bis 1315325 proves. The damage was inflicted on the jet during the ace's 6 October 1951 clash with the 4th FW

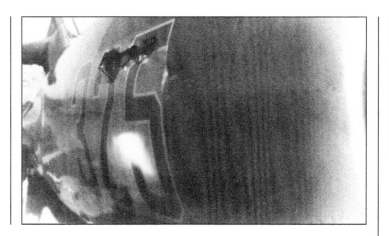

With his ejection seat badly damaged, the pilot of F-86A 49-1319 was forced to crash-land his fighter on a beach 13 km west of Pyongyang. He was quickly rescued by a US Navy helicopter, but his Sabre fell into North Korean hands

just behind its instrument panel and the Sabre dived for the ground. I didn't follow him, as after such a punishing hit from the cannon I knew that the fighter was doomed.'

The Sabre pilot was unable to escape because of a damaged ejector seat, so, with his fighter trailing black smoke and its engine barely capable of keeping the jet aloft, he limped off towards the Gulf of Korea. The 4th FW pilot did not get too far, however, being forced to crash-land on a beach 13 km (eight miles) west of Pyongyang. He was quickly rescued by helicopter, and his disabled Sabre fell into communist hands.

INSUFFICIENT STRENGTH

The MiG regiments' success in forcing UN attack aircraft to operate south of the Chongchon River meant that Chinese army units could now be resupplied more easily. Nevertheless, fighter-bombers remained active over North Korea, and 64th IAK did not have sufficient strength to force them to move further south. The 4th FW (two F-86 squadrons in Korea and one in reserve in Japan), 49th and 136th FBGs (six F-84 squadrons in total), 8th and 51st FBGs (five F-80 squadrons), 18th FBG (three F-51D squadrons) and No 77 Sqn RAAF (Meteor F 8s) faced five MiG-equipped IAPs. On occasion, US Navy/Marine Corps and Royal Navy fighter-bombers also ventured into areas patrolled by the MiG-15s too.

On paper, 64th IAK fielded 150 aircraft, but in practice it was rather less than this. Numerically, every UN squadron was approximately equal to one Soviet IAP. Aside from the USAF/RAAF fighters and fighter-bombers, the enemy also had three B-29 bomber groups (nine squadrons, totalling 100 aircraft) and two B-26 groups to call on.

During the engagements fought in 1950-51, the MiGs were usually flown by Soviet pilots, with Chinese and North Korean aviators taking part in combat operations somewhat unwillingly because a lack of training made them vulnerable to the better-trained UN pilots. A further constraint was the limited number of airfields available for operations by the Soviet fighters. Restricted to flying from Antung and Tatung-kao, the MiG regiments could only realistically protect communist troops north of the Chongchon River because their jets lacked sufficient fuel to intercept aircraft flying further south.

Furthermore, for political reasons Soviet pilots were forbidden from patrolling south of the Pyongyang-Vonsan line. And even if they had been allowed to venture over UN-held territory, their MiG-15s had insufficient fuel reserves to permit pilots to engage in low-altitude dogfights with fighter-bombers and then return to base.

Forcing fighter-bombers away from the Chongchon River area was considered to be the first step in establishing air supremacy over the whole of northern Korea. Such supremacy would in turn allow advanced airfields to be established in the recovered territory from which the MiGs could put up a more effective aerial umbrella over Chinese supply routes that stretched as far south as the frontline. Moreover, they could protect Chinese Tu-2s and North Korean Il-10s, which would finally get the chance to attack enemy logistics. Indeed, UN ground forces had not had to contend with attack from the air since July 1950, when the Korean People's Army air forces were virtually chased from the sky.

In early October 1951, UN reconnaissance aircraft began bringing back photographs showing nearly 18 completed airfields in North Korea. Three of them – Namsi, Thachon and Saamchan – became priority targets for the USAF, but the task of eliminating them appeared to be beyond the fighter-bomber units, and the Sabre squadrons which would have to escort them. On the other hand, a squadron of B-29s possessed the striking power of a wing of fighter-bombers. Knocking out these bases as quickly as possible became the primary mission for Headquarters, FEAF, and it turned to the B-29 groups to achieve this. Despite their vulnerability, the four-engined bombers would have to perform a series of large-scale daylight raids deep into enemy territory.

On Monday, 22 October, 19th BG Superfortresses opened what was to be a black week in USAF history with massive, simultaneous, attacks on several targets. And while the B-29s were striking at Thachon airfield, F-80 and F-84 fighter-bombers hit railway stations in the Sukchon-Anju-Sunchon area. At 1503 hrs, 303rd IAD was given the order to scramble, its mission being to intercept the raiders, although the location of the B-29s was not yet clear to Corps Headquarters. As the situation clarified, however, 17th and 523rd IAPs joined battle with the attacking fighter-bombers, while 14 MiGs from 18th GvIAP, which had climbed to 10,000 m (32,500 ft), were directed towards the B-29s. 18th GvIAP ace Lt Col Aleksander Smorchkov recalled;

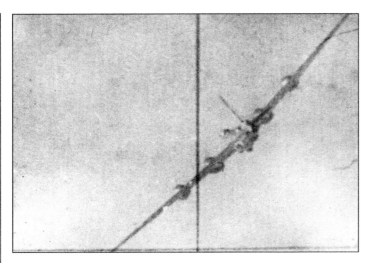

This B-29 from the 307th BW was caught by the camera gun of Lt Col Smorchkov's MiG-15 on 23 October – 'Black Tuesday'. 64th IAK credited Smorchkov's 18th GvIAP with three Superfortresses and three Thunderjets destroyed following this epic aerial battle. Smorchkov's overall tally of 12 kills in Korea included three B-29s destroyed

'These B-29 missions were the most difficult sorties I flew in Korea. We took off in adverse weather, and some of my pilots had little experience of flying in such conditions. We looked for breaks in the clouds, but by the time we reached 10,000 m (32,500 ft) the sky had become overcast. Then we received the order to follow a course that would take us to the "big ones". We had to lose 5000 m (16,000 ft) of altitude and fly under clouds. But how could we find them through the overcast? I could do it on my own, but I had the whole IAP with me. I couldn't ask my base because they would expect me to be able to manage, and I might even be reprimanded for asking such a question.

'I looked behind me and saw the whole regiment there, holding formation well. I ordered them all to put their noses down, to pay attention and not to close up in the clouds. I could see my wingman but nothing in front of me. I didn't want any collisions! I was their CO, and therefore had responsibility for all my pilots. If just one pair collided it would be my fault. But we began to break out of the clouds and the overcast was above us. And there they were – B-29s, just three kilometres (two miles) from us. Our command post estimated that there were 12 bombers – I'd already counted them – and up to 120 escorting fighters.

'What about my regiment? I looked around and there they were! All of them were with me, and I felt better at once. I ordered them to go for the big boys, but not to forget the small ones. So we went into the attack. The speed of our targets was 500 kmh (312mph) and ours was 1100 kmh (688 mph). The escorting pilots appeared to be cowards. If we forced them into a pair or a group of four aircraft, they flew apart, right and left, leaving us with a clear path to the bombers. "Good", I thought. "These guys are working for us".

'I fired a burst at one bomber and saw my tracer rounds miss the target. As I got closer, I fired again at its right-hand engines and fuel tank. Red flames came from them and the Superfortress started to go down. As it began to break up, I saw six parachutes opening, but there was no time for me to watch, as the escorts seemed to have woken up.

'I had always taught my pilots that an aircraft like a B-29 was worth all their ammunition. If each of us could bring down a Superfortress, then that would be great. But I still had some ammunition left after downing my bomber, so I used it to destroy an F-84. I said to my wingman, Vladimir Voistinnyh, "Go ahead and I'll cover you", as he went after a Thunderjet, but the battle was fading away by then and we were ordered home.'

Pilots of 18th GvIAP were credited with downing three B-29s and three F-84s, with Smorchkov claiming one of each. Initially, however, only his bomber kill was confirmed. The other pilots reported that they had indeed shot down two more B-29s, although the bombers managed to remain in formation despite being hit – the USAF confirmed the loss of a single B-29, but no F-84s were destroyed.

'BLACK TUESDAY'

The following day, 23 October 1951, was to go down in the history of the Korean War as 'Black Tuesday'. For the MiG-15 pilots, operations commenced between 0910-0930 hrs, when 64th IAK radars detected eight groups of enemy aircraft approaching North Korea. All told, there were up to 200 fighters and fighter-bombers (F-86s, F-84s, F-80s and Meteors), plus a group of B-29 bombers, heading for the newly built airfield targets.

From 0935 hrs until 1004 hrs, the fighter-bombers delivered concentrated strikes in the Anju area. The B-29s, meanwhile, concentrated on bombing Namsi airfield, although some ordnance fell two kilometres south of the base. Between 0924-0933 hrs, 303rd IAD scrambled 20 MiGs-15bis from 17th IAP under the command of Maj Maslennikov (four Korean War kills), 20 MiGs-15bis from 18th GvIAP, led by Lt Col A P Smorchkov, and 18 from 523rd IAP, commanded by Maj D P Oskin (future 15-kill ace). A further 26 fighters from 176th and 196th IAPs of 324th IAD took off at around 0945 hrs.

303rd IAD's tactical formation consisted of a single attack group made up of fighters from 18th GvIAP and 523rd IAP, with 17th IAP providing cover. The primary attack formation flew in line astern, with Smorchkov in overall command. 324th IAD MiGs were to keep the enemy fighters occupied, thus leaving 303rd IAD jets free to go after the bombers.

At 1040 hrs 18th GvIAP, leading the attacking group, encountered 30 Sabres. At the same time Smorchkov sighted ten B-29s, escorted by 36 Thunderjets. Fourteen MiGs of the 1st and 3rd Squadrons were ordered to engage the enemy fighters, while a group of six from the 2nd Squadron, led by Smorchkov, attacked the bombers. In the ensuing battle Smorchkov and Capt N L Kornienko (five Korean War victories) claimed to have destroyed two B-29s, while Snr Lt Chukin got an F-84. Two MiGs were slightly damaged by the Thunderjets.

At 1043 hrs, 523rd IAP joined the fray. Its pilots had to fight the bombers as well as the escorting Sabres, Thunderjets and Meteors. Following a series of ferocious engagements, the regiment's pilots claimed five B-29s and one F-84 shot down. Dmitriy Oskin was credited with the destruction of two Superfortresses while Capt Stepan Bakhaev (11 kills in Korea) got one.

Two minutes after the 523rd IAP pilots entered the battle, they were joined by 17th IAP. Its 2nd and 3rd Squadrons engaged the fighters, while the 1st Squadron attacked the bombers. Vasiliy Shulev scored his

Brimmed hats were popular amongst Soviet MiG pilots serving with 64th IAK in the Korean War if the photographs in this chapter are anything to go by! Here, aces Lt Col Aleksander Smorchkov and 523rd IAP CO Maj Dmitriy Oskin (15 kills) model their favourite head wear. These two pilots were credited with shooting down five B-29s between 22 and 24 October 1951

fourth victory – over an F-84 – while Snr Lts Nikolaev (three Korean victories), Bykov (also three) and Capt Bychkov (five) were each credited with bringing down a B-29. Nikolaev's MiG was holed by defensive fire when he pressed home his attack on a B-29.

324th IAD pilots did not attack the bombers, as they stuck to their job of keeping the escorting Sabre and Shooting Star units busy.

Again, claims by the Soviet pilots failed to tally with official USAF losses on 23 October. Three B-29As from the 307th BW were indeed downed, as was a solitary F-84E from the 111th FBS. The MiG units were credited with ten Superfortresses and three Thunderjets destroyed. Admittedly, apart from the three bombers that crashed near Namsi and Cinnampo, four more had to be written off after performing emergency landings at South Korean bases. And three B-29s that made it back to Okinawa were so badly damaged by the MiGs that they were scrapped.

F-84 and F-86 pilots and B-29 gunners were credited with having brought down six MiG-15s on the 23rd, although the Soviets reported that no fighters were lost. Indeed, it appears that only three jets suffered minor battle damage.

Despite the mauling the bombers had received on 'Black Tuesday', they returned to the fray the following day. This time the target for eight B-29s was a railway bridge near Sonchon. Sabres flew a fighter screening patrol near the Yalu River, Australian Meteors flew offensive sweeps in the bombers' area of operation and Thunderjets also performed close escort for the Superfortresses.

All three regiments of 303rd IAD took off and set course for Anju under Smorchkov's command. The plan was that 523rd IAP would keep the escorting fighters busy while 17th IAP and 18th GvIAP broke through to attack the bombers, but by the time the MiGs reached the target area the B-29s had already dropped their ordnance and were heading for Korea Bay. At 1522 hrs 523rd IAP encountered the covering Meteors and Sabres and a battle developed in the Sunchon area.

In an effort to chase down the Superfortresses, the MiG pilots of 18th GvIAP flew southeast until, at 1535 hrs, the pilots found a group of B-29s escorted by Meteors, Thunderjets and Sabres. Smorchkov decided that the 1st Squadron would engage the enemy fighters while the 2nd and 3rd Squadrons attacked the bombers.

This encounter took place close to the Pyongyang-Vonsan line, which 64th IAK crews had orders not to cross – each pilot only had time for one attack on the Superfortresses. Most opened fire too far away from the B-29s (between 1.5 and 2 km), and the only effective attack was made by Smorchkov, who closed to within 700 m (750 yrd) of his target before firing his guns. He broke off his attack when the range had come down to 300 m (325 yrd), by which point the bomber had burst into flames.

17th IAP pilots failed to reach the B-29s prior to the bombers crossing the Pyongyang-Vonsan line.

This engagement saw more losses inflicted on UN forces, with MiG pilots from 18th and 523rd IAPs claiming four F-86s, four Meteors and one B-29 destroyed for the loss of a single jet from the latter regiment, whose pilot was forced to eject after battling with the Sabres. The USAF did indeed lose a single B-29A from the 98th BG on this date, as well as two F-86s, and claimed two MiGs destroyed (one was credited to the 4th FW

Dressed in civilian attire, deputy CO of 18th GvIAP Lt Col Aleksander Smorchkov and 17th IAP CO Lt Col Grigoriy Pulov (eight Korean War victories) prepare to enjoy a spot of leave in the autumn of 1951

and the other to the 98th BG). According to RAAF records, no Meteors were shot down, however.

Lt Col A P Smorchkov had been particularly successful during the anti-B-29 operations of 22-24 October, having been credited with victories over Boeing bombers on three consecutive days – an extremely rare occurrence in the Korean War. Astonishingly, all his Superfortress kills matched losses suffered by the USAF. Smorchkov was made a HSU by month-end for his outstanding efforts in combat.

These three pilots all saw combat with 196th IAP in 1951-52. They are, from left to right, regimental navigating officer Capt Tkatskiy, deputy regimental CO Maj A I Mitusov (five World War 2 victories and seven in the Korean War) and flight leader Capt L N Ivanov (seven Korean War kills)

On 26 October Snr Lt Fedor Shebanov of 196th IAP became the first Soviet ace to be shot down and killed by enemy fighters. He and his wingman were flying over cloud when they were attacked at long range by fighters that the latter identified as Shooting Stars (although no F-80 pilots claimed kills on this date, two MiGs were credited to F-86s from the 4th FW). As the wingman pulled up and climbed away from his attacker, he saw Shebanov's MiG going down into the clouds – the ace was never seen again. A search party sent to the area subsequently found the burned out wreck of Shebanov's MiG fighter.

Saturday, 27 October, was the final day of 'Black Week', and once again B-29s headed into North Korea on a bold daylight mission when nine bombers attacked a railway bridge in the Anju area. The Superfortresses were escorted by a mixed formation of 32 Shooting Stars and Thunderjets.

The USAF knew full well by now that MiG pilots avoided flying over open water whenever possible, so the mission planners plotted a route that kept the B-29s over the Yellow Sea for as long as possible, before crossing the coast just short of the target. As had by now become customary, a Sabre screening patrol flew over the Yalu River ahead of the main bomber formation.

At 1004 hrs, 22 MiG-15s from 523rd IAP, 303rd IAD, led by HSU Lt Col Aleksander Karasyov, took off to intercept the B-29s. Karasyov, who had become 64th IAK's 12th ace on 19 September 1951, had flown 380 combat sorties, fought in 112 aerial battles and scored 30 individual and 11 group kills during World War 2. He would add seven more victories to his tally over Korea.

17th IAP and 18th GvIAP also scrambled groups of 20 fighters that were tasked with engaging the screening patrol while 523rd IAP went for the bombers. Ten-kill ace Snr Lt Dmitriy Samoylov was flying one of the 22 MiGs sortied by the latter regiment, and he remembered;

'My wingman was Snr Lt Mikhail Zykov, and we were led by our 2nd Squadron commander (and future five-kill ace) Capt V P Popov. The 1st and 3rd Squadrons were to attack the bombers and our unit would engage the fighters, but when we sighted the Superfortresses, we found that they were wide open to attack – there was no escort. I said to Popov, "We should probably target the big ones", so he ordered us all to "Attack!" and

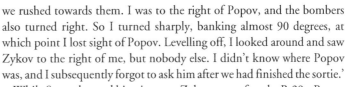

we rushed towards them. I was to the right of Popov, and the bombers also turned right. So I turned sharply, banking almost 90 degrees, at which point I lost sight of Popov. Levelling off, I looked around and saw Zykov to the right of me, but nobody else. I didn't know where Popov was, and I subsequently forgot to ask him after we had finished the sortie.'

While Samoylov and his wingman Zykov went after the B-29s, Popov and the remaining four 2nd Squadron MiGs engaged the escorting F-84s. Indeed, Dmitri Samoylov and his wingman had been the only ones in his unit that had managed to break through to the Super-fortresses. He continued;

'There were nine B-29 bombers in front of me. Their engines were smoking, as they were obviously running for Korea Bay at full throttle because they knew we wouldn't follow them out over the sea. But I was flying at more than 1000 kmh (625 mph) and they were travelling at less than 700 kmh (440 mph), so we closed very quickly. They fired their machine guns at us, and although I couldn't see the tracer rounds heading for me, I knew they were targeting us because I could see flashes from the turrets. I attacked a bomber and set it on fire.

'My speed was still high, but I could have turned round for a head-on attack. I found that it was better to come in from behind, however, as the closing speed wasn't so high. As I stopped firing I began a climbing turn, which took me almost over the group. Then Zykov cried "I'm hit!" and that was it – if one of us was hit we had to break off the fight. Turning away, we saw the whole mass of MiGs and F-84s flying towards the Superfortresses. I caught one Thunderjet head-on. It was easy. I fired a burst and saw him fall. After returning home we examined Zykov's aircraft – it had suffered a solitary hole in the fuselage.'

In the wake of this mission 523rd IAP pilots were credited with shoot-ing down two B-29s and two F-84s. In addition, 17th IAP and 18th GvIAP claimed two F-86s and an F-84 – officially, USAF losses on this date amounted to a solitary B-29A from the 19th BG. All the MiGs returned from the mission (three had been damaged by fire from F-84s), despite B-29 gunners claiming to have downed five of them, with a sixth being credited to the 4th FW.

The clash between MiG-15s and B-29s on 27 October proved to be the last time that the two types fought each other in daylight over

Pictured at Tatung-kao airfield in November 1951, 523rd IAP regimental CO Maj Dmitriy Oskin (left) and two unidentified aviators are kept amused by the antics of squadron leader Capt Grigoriy Okhay (six World War 2 victories and 11 Korean War kills) and his pet monkey

North Korea. The following day, senior bomber commanders attended a high-level meeting at Fifth Air Force HQ at Itazuke air base. They concluded that even raising the number of escorting fighters would not be enough to stop the MiGs from breaking through and attacking the vulnerable Superfortresses.

Under these circumstances, the CO of FEAF Bomber Command, Brig Gen Joe W Kelly, suggested that the attacks should be made at night. Gen Otto P Weyland, Commander of the FEAF, agreed with him. The end result of this meeting was that Superfortresses would no longer fly north of Pyongyang. The MiG-15 pilots of 64th IAK had put a stop to the daylight career of the B-29 strategic bomber force in the Korean War. The battles between Superfortress crews and MiG pilots were to be fought at night from now on.

And 64th IAK had already commenced night operations over Korea, as 351st IAP had been flying nocturnal missions from Antung since 9 September. The regiment, directly subordinated to the corps commander, was equipped with 30 piston-engined La-11 fighters. Capt Simko opened 351st IAP's Korean combat score during the night of 12/13 October when he was credited with shooting down a B-26 (USAF records fail to indicate such a loss). He also claimed to have damaged a second Invader on the 21st.

In all, 64th IAK pilots scored 92 victories during October 1951, with 16 B-29s, one B-26, 41 F-86s, 21 F-84s, 12 F-80s and a carrier-borne piston-engined aircraft (probably an F4U) being credited to the Soviet airmen. Ten pilots had claimed their fifth victories during the month, while corps losses numbered eight jets and three pilots. USAF fighter pilots and B-29 gunners claimed to have downed 37 MiG-15s, however.

PEPELYAEV TO THE FORE

November 1951 was to be the most productive month in terms of aerial victories for 196th IAP CO Lt Col Evgeniy Pepelyaev, who would be credited with scoring six kills that month. The first of these successes came just after noon on the 8th, when Pepelyaev led three squadrons to intercept enemy fighters and fighter-bombers heading for the North Korean capital. In the ensuing dogfight near Pyongyang, he latched onto the tail of a Sabre and opened fire with all his guns. The 4th FW jet literally disintegrated under the weight of Pepelyaev's fire.

Later that same day, while leading two squadrons to intercept fighter-bombers attacking trains in the Anju area, Pepelyaev and his wingman attacked eight F-84 fighters, one of which was shot down by the Soviet ace (USAF records confirm the loss of an F-86A, but not an F-84).

On 27 November Lt Col Pepelyaev claimed another Thunderjet kill (USAF records state an F-80C was lost to MiGs and an F-84E hit the ground while strafing a train). The following day he shot down two F-86s (one F-86E loss was listed by the USAF), with another Sabre destroyed on the 29th (USAF records state a possible loss of a 4th FW aircraft to MiG-15s on this date).

Some 24 MiG-15s from all three squadrons in 196th IAP had taken off at 1338 hrs on the 29th after enemy fighters were detected over the Yalu River. As Pepelyaev and his wingman, Snr Lt Ryzhkov (who scored four victories over Korea), neared Pyongyang, they were attacked by a lone

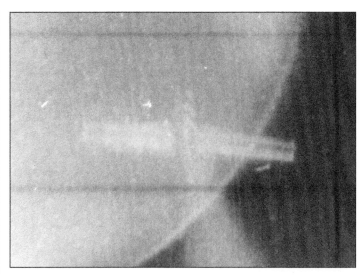

Lt Col Evgeniy Pepelyaev engages F-86A-5 50-0673 of the 4th FW's 336th FS at a range of 140 m on 28 November 1951. The jet is clearly trailing white smoke, which is probably kerosene leaking from a ruptured wing centre section tank

The groundcrew of 351st IAP squadron leader Maj Dushin (one victory in China and two in the Korean War) prepare his La-11 for a night combat sortie in November 1951. The propeller spinner, engine cowling and side number are painted red, the uppersurfaces light grey and the undersides black

Sabre. Both pilots avoided it by making a climbing turn, and the regimental CO soon got onto the Sabre's tail. The American pilot tried to escape Pepelyaev's attentions with a series of descending rolls, but he failed. Firing several long bursts from all three of his guns, the Soviet ace reported seeing strikes on the Sabre's fuselage before it went down.

Pepelyaev and his wingman overshot the doomed F-86 as it lost altitude, despite having deployed their air brakes. The squadron's second pair, comprising Capt B V Bokach (six kills in Korea) and Lt Frolov, duly followed the Sabre down so as to finish it off if necessary, but they reported seeing it crash into a hill and explode.

By the end of November Pepelyaev had increased his tally to 14 victories, all of which were fighters – ten F-86s, two F-84s and two 'F-94 Starfires' (actually F9F Panthers).

As previously mentioned in this chapter, B-29s switched to night operations in November, and on several occasions they encountered La-11s flown by pilots of 351st IAP. One such clash took place on 16 November, and resulted in Capt Dushin being credited with a victory (no loss was recorded by the USAF).

Other engagements with B-29s that month were unsuccessful, although on the 28th Capts Karelin and Golyshevsky managed to hit a Superfortress. 351st IAP pilots fired at it from long range and the bomber was listed as damaged.

By the end of November, Soviet pilots had been credited with 70 kills – a tally which included one B-29, 27 F-86s, 31 F-84s, nine F-80s and two carrier-borne aircraft, which were probably Corsairs or Skyraiders. Another four pilots had reached five victories. Ten MiGs had been lost, with one pilot missing and four killed. Among the latter was ace Capt German Shatalov of 523rd IAP, who was shot down on the 28th by an F-86. His victory tally stood at two F-51s, one F-80 and two F-86s at the time of his demise. USAF and US Navy fighter pilots claimed 18 MiG-15s destroyed in November 1951.

MiG-15 aces surround the grave of Capt Timofeev of 523rd IAP at Port Arthur, in Manchuria, in May 1953. Timofeev had scored four victories in the Korean War prior to being killed during a dogfight on 28 November 1951. Pictured flanking his headstone are (from left to right) Maj V P Popov (five Korean War victories), Lt Col Maslennikov (three victories), HSU Col A N Karasev (30 individual and 11 group victories during World War 2, plus seven more in the Korean War), HSU Lt Col D P Oskin (15 Korean War victories) and HSU Lt Col G I Pulov (eight Korean War victories)

MiGs Versus Meteors

On 1 December 1951, the RAAF's No 77 Sqn, equipped with Meteor F 8s, suffered a major defeat. The unit had regularly fought MiG-15s since it had swapped Mustangs for Meteors five months earlier, and although Soviet pilots had claimed numerous F 8 kills, only one jet had actually been downed (on 29 August) by 64th IAK to date. This all changed on the morning of 1 December, however.

Fourteen Meteors had departed No 77 Sqn's Kimpo base with orders to fly a screening patrol. Two F 8s then split off from the main formation and were held in an orbit over the Pyongyang area, relaying radio messages between the remaining jets and Kimpo. Three more Meteors also broke away from the primary group to make a run over the Yalu.

At 0925 hrs 64th IAK radar stations detected more than 100 enemy aircraft flying in seven groups bound for Daiwato and Sinbito. The communists were concerned that these machines could pose a serious threat to the Antung air base complex if they attacked from the sea, so fighters from 176th GvIAP were scrambled at 0944 hrs in order to head them off. This group, totalling 20 MiG-15s, was led by Lt Col Sergey Vishnyakov (six Korean War victories).

After five minutes in the air, the MiG pilots received information from the ground that a group of 16 enemy aircraft were some 200 km (125 miles) away, heading in the general direction of Antung at a height of 7000 m (23,000 ft). The pilots of 176th GvIAP were ordered to intercept these aircraft in the Anju area. The MiGs quickly split up into an attack group, commanded by Vishnayakov, and a covering group led by 13-kill MiG ace Capt Sergey Kramarenko. The pilots soon found the enemy fighters – No 77 Sqn's Meteor F 8s – in four elements of four aircraft near Sonchon.

Sizing up the situation, Vishnyakov decided to attack by deploying all his aircraft against both Australian flanks. Kramarenko and his wingman, Snr Lt Guloy, went after the pair of Meteors on the outer right-hand side of the formation towards the rear, as the ace later recalled;

'I saw the enemy to the left, some five to ten kilometres (3-6 miles) away from us. Our group began a right turn. We then dived down to attack them, dropping behind the Australians. I ordered, "Attack!" We closed in on the rear flight of Meteors. I ordered my wingman to "Take the right one – the left one is mine!" I opened fire and saw my shell bursts dancing all over the enemy aircraft. Its right engine flamed. I noticed the Meteor wingman's tail flying off as the result of a burst from my wingman. We passed over the falling aircraft and went into a steep climb.

'As I looked around me, the battle literally surrounded us. Our MiGs were shooting at the Glosters. The Australians spread out and single aircraft were left on their own. Now there were eight left out of sixteen aircraft. I saw a Meteor leaving the battle. We overtook him and attacked. Seeing us, the Australian turned, but too slowly. I managed to frame him in my sights and opened fire. My shells burst on the Meteor's wings and the pilot bailed out. Then I noticed another Meteor hurrying back to his comrades. I was nearly out of ammunition, so I ordered my wingman to "Attack!" But his speed was too high and he overshot. I decided to let the Meteor pilot fly home and tell them all about the battle – two kills were enough for me. We turned back and headed for our airfield.'

The engagement had lasted nine minutes. By the end of it, the pilots of 176th GvIAP had claimed nine victories, although in reality the Australians had lost three F 8s – the remaining fighters had managed to dive away from the MiGs when they launched their attack. Three Meteors had failed to return and two pilots had been captured and one killed. All the Soviet fighters returned safely to Antung, although No 77 Sqn was credited with downing two MiGs. This action effectively ended the Meteor's career as a frontline fighter, with the RAAF squadron switching to the ground attack mission early in the New Year.

On the day of the Australian defeat, the USAF's 51st FW made its combat debut with the F-86E Sabre in Korea. At that time, two of the group's three squadrons were based at Suwon, with the third held in reserve in Japan. The 4th FW now had three squadrons in Korea, however, as its third had arrived at Kimpo from Johnson AFB, Japan, in mid-November. By December 1951, therefore, the USAF had deployed 127 F-86 fighters, split between five squadrons, to South Korean bases, with an additional 38 Sabres being held in reserve in Japan. UN fighter strength had increased threefold in just a matter of months.

Such an increase in numbers had an immediate effect on the outcome of engagements fought with the MiGs, and 64th IAK pilots found it much harder to break through screening patrols flown by F-86s charged with protecting the vulnerable fighter-bombers. This caused a fall in the MiG kill tally for December, although Soviet pilots still managed to claim 83 enemy aircraft destroyed – 54 F-86s, 12 F-84s, eight F-80s and nine Meteors. 64th IAK also added eight new aces to its roster.

In previous months fighters had represented about 40 per cent of the corps' total score, with the remainder being fighter-bombers, but in December that situation was reversed. The proportion of Sabres shot down rose to 65 per cent, thus reflecting the greater number of F-86s now in-theatre. Soviet losses had also fallen, with just six MiGs failing to return to base in December. Two pilots were killed. USAF and RAAF pilots claimed 35 MiGs destroyed, however.

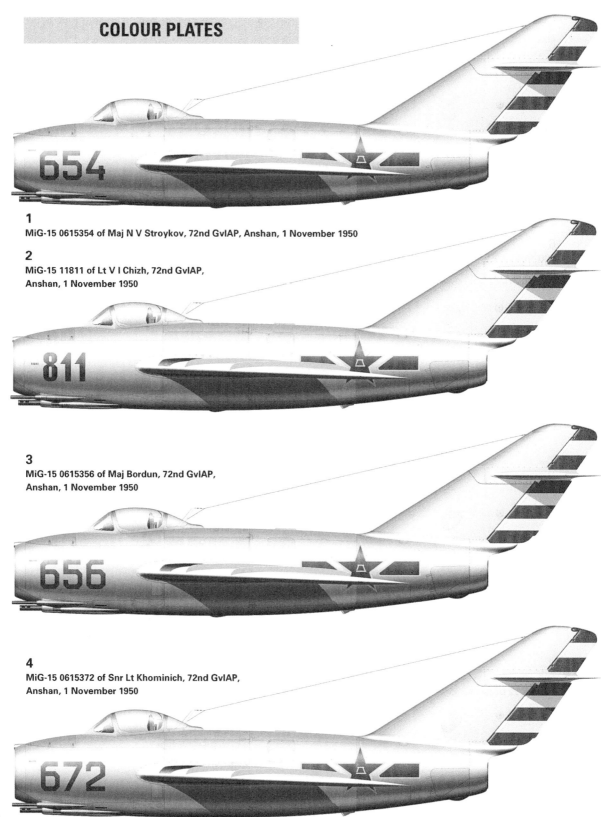

1
MiG-15 0615354 of Maj N V Stroykov, 72nd GvIAP, Anshan, 1 November 1950

2
MiG-15 11811 of Lt V I Chizh, 72nd GvIAP,
Anshan, 1 November 1950

3
MiG-15 0615356 of Maj Bordun, 72nd GvIAP,
Anshan, 1 November 1950

4
MiG-15 0615372 of Snr Lt Khominich, 72nd GvIAP,
Anshan, 1 November 1950

5
MiG-15 0615334 of Maj V I Kolyadin, 28th GvIAP, Mukden-West, November 1950

6
MiG-15 120125 of Capt Grachyov, 139th GvIAP,
Liaoyang, 9 November 1950

7
MiG-15bis 0715323 of Capt S I Naumenko, 29th GvIAP,
Antung, January 1951

8
MiG-15bis 0615396 of Capt Nikolay Vorobyov, 177th IAP,
Antung, 22 December 1950

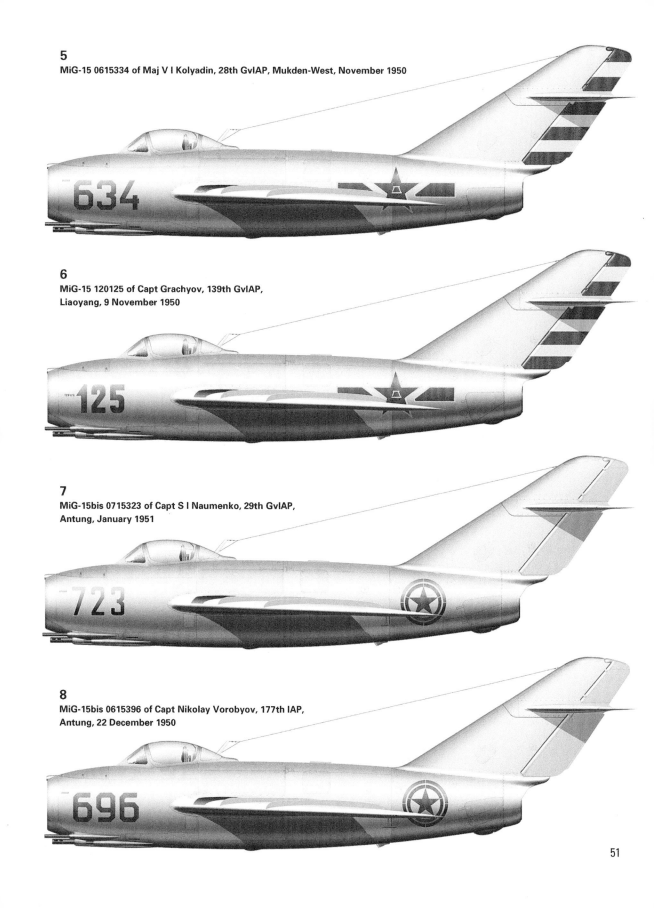

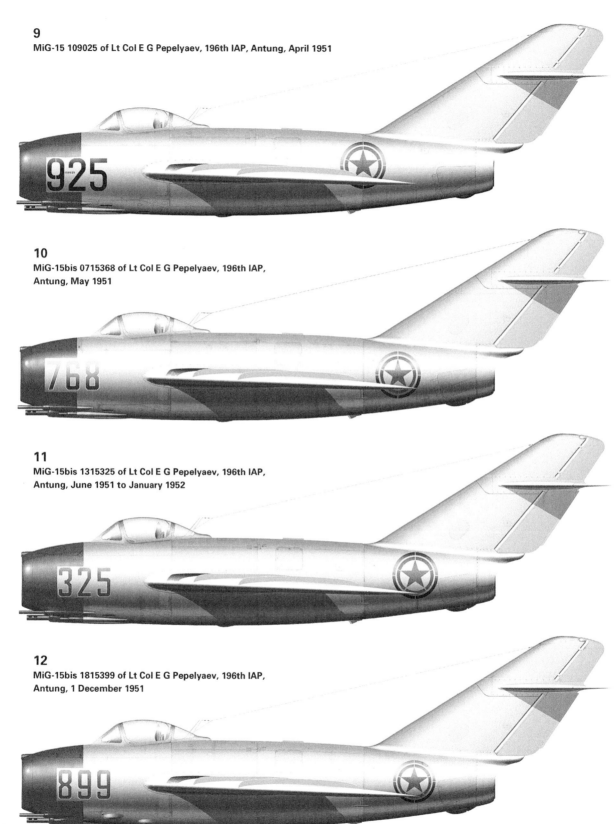

9
MiG-15 109025 of Lt Col E G Pepelyaev, 196th IAP, Antung, April 1951

10
MiG-15bis 0715368 of Lt Col E G Pepelyaev, 196th IAP,
Antung, May 1951

11
MiG-15bis 1315325 of Lt Col E G Pepelyaev, 196th IAP,
Antung, June 1951 to January 1952

12
MiG-15bis 1815399 of Lt Col E G Pepelyaev, 196th IAP,
Antung, 1 December 1951

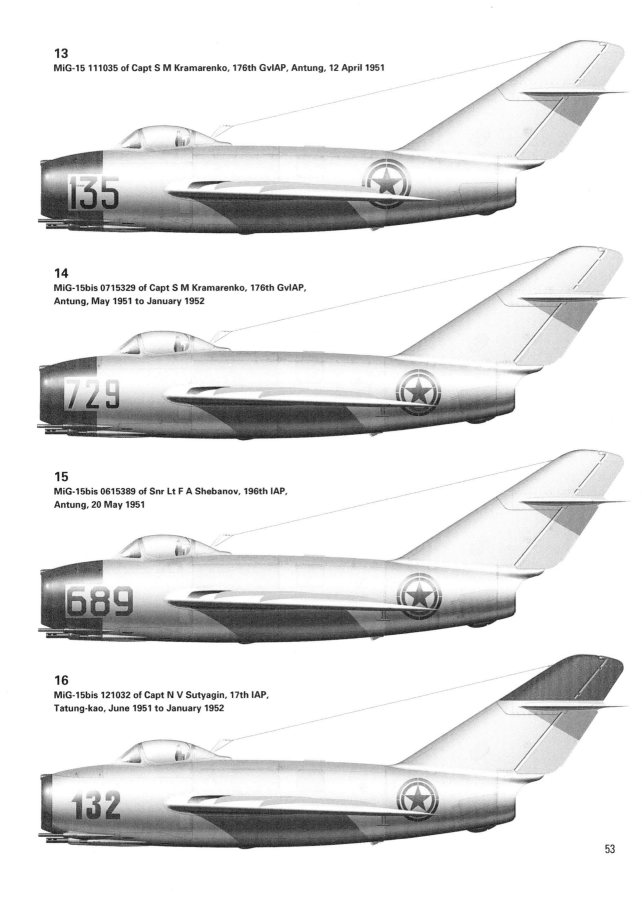

13
MiG-15 111035 of Capt S M Kramarenko, 176th GvIAP, Antung, 12 April 1951

14
MiG-15bis 0715329 of Capt S M Kramarenko, 176th GvIAP,
Antung, May 1951 to January 1952

15
MiG-15bis 0615389 of Snr Lt F A Shebanov, 196th IAP,
Antung, 20 May 1951

16
MiG-15bis 121032 of Capt N V Sutyagin, 17th IAP,
Tatung-kao, June 1951 to January 1952

17
MiG-15bis 121067 of Snr Lt D A Samoylov, 523rd IAP,
Tatung-kao, June 1951 to January 1952

18
MiG-15bis 123045 of Lt Col A P Smorchkov, 18th GvIAP,
Tatung-kao, May 1951 to January 1952

19
MiG-15bis 123051 of Maj D P Oskin, 18th GvIAP,
Tatung-kao, September 1951

20
MiG-15bis 121026 of Capt N G Dokashenko, 17th IAP,
Tatung-kao, late January 1952

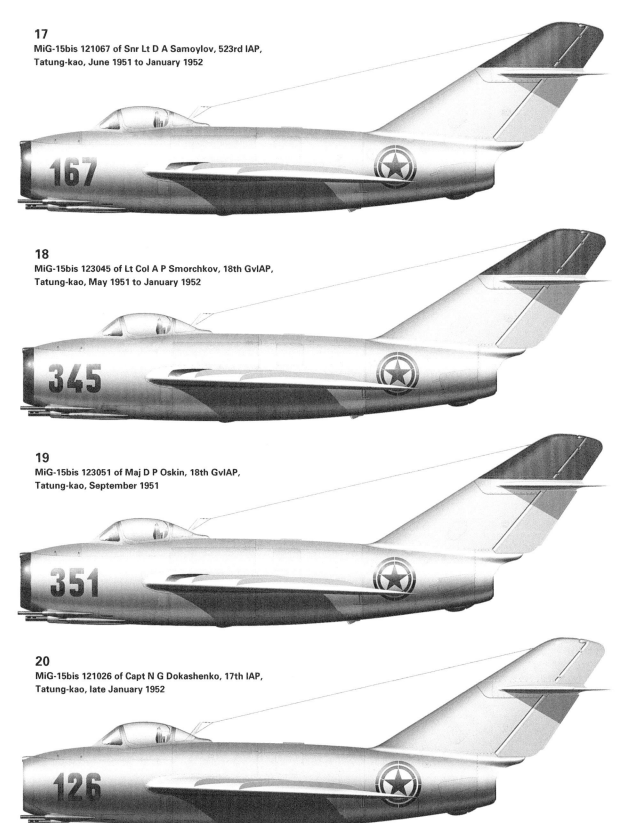

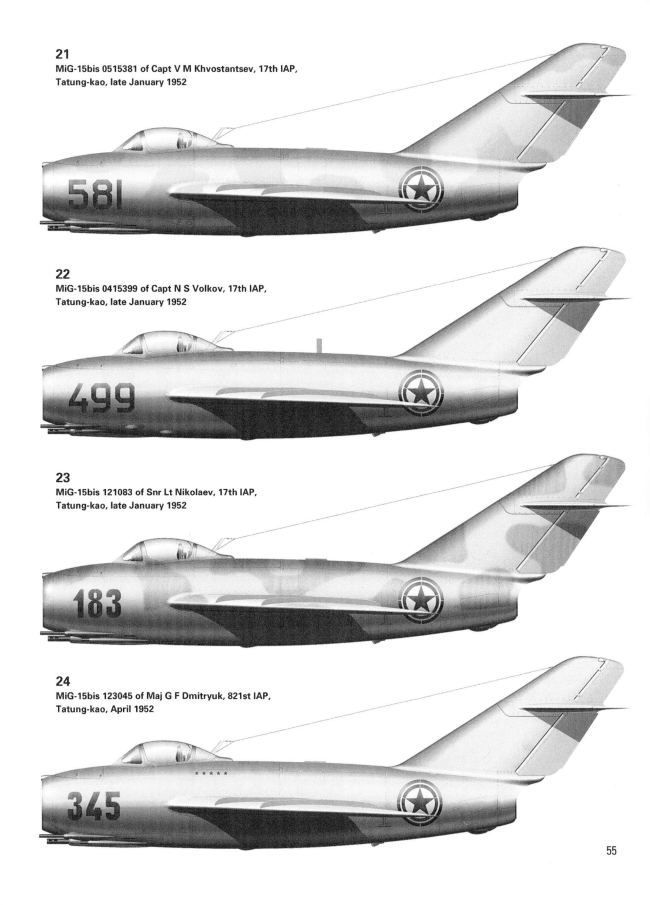

21
MiG-15bis 0515381 of Capt V M Khvostantsev, 17th IAP,
Tatung-kao, late January 1952

22
MiG-15bis 0415399 of Capt N S Volkov, 17th IAP,
Tatung-kao, late January 1952

23
MiG-15bis 121083 of Snr Lt Nikolaev, 17th IAP,
Tatung-kao, late January 1952

24
MiG-15bis 123045 of Maj G F Dmitryuk, 821st IAP,
Tatung-kao, April 1952

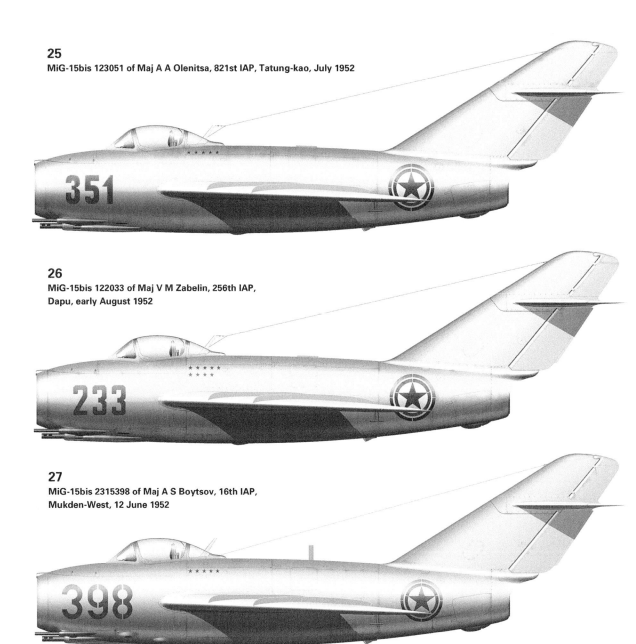

25
MiG-15bis 123051 of Maj A A Olenitsa, 821st IAP, Tatung-kao, July 1952

26
MiG-15bis 122033 of Maj V M Zabelin, 256th IAP,
Dapu, early August 1952

27
MiG-15bis 2315398 of Maj A S Boytsov, 16th IAP,
Mukden-West, 12 June 1952

28
MiG-15bis 2415308 of Maj P V Minervin, 16th IAP,
Mukden-West, May 1952

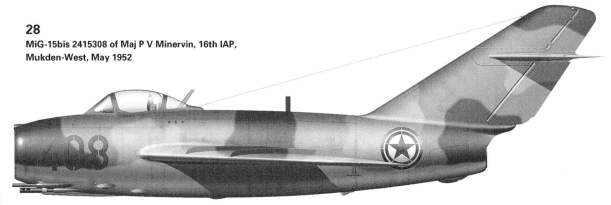

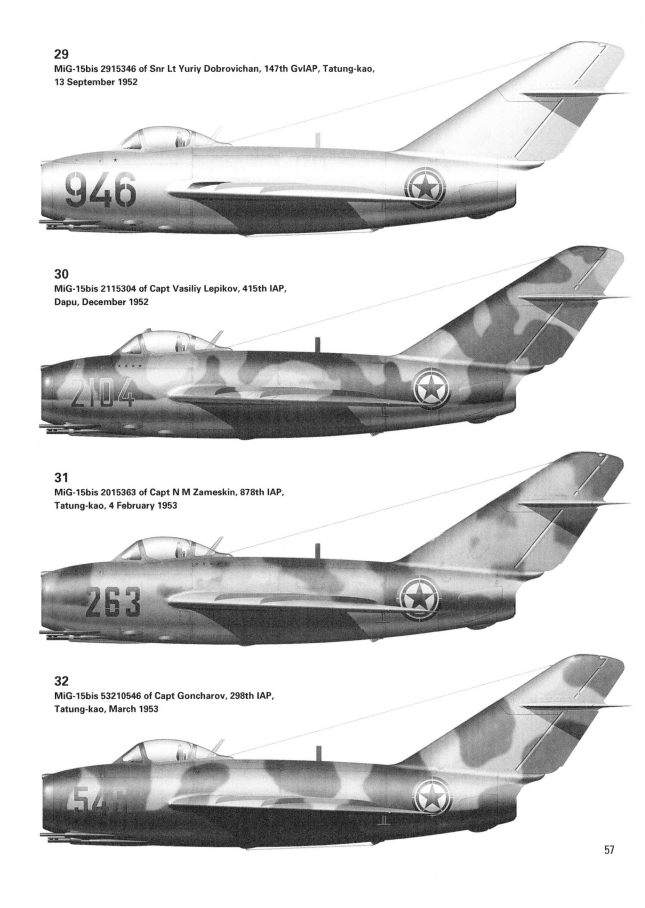

29
MiG-15bis 2915346 of Snr Lt Yuriy Dobrovichan, 147th GvIAP, Tatung-kao,
13 September 1952

30
MiG-15bis 2115304 of Capt Vasiliy Lepikov, 415th IAP,
Dapu, December 1952

31
MiG-15bis 2015363 of Capt N M Zameskin, 878th IAP,
Tatung-kao, 4 February 1953

32
MiG-15bis 53210546 of Capt Goncharov, 298th IAP,
Tatung-kao, March 1953

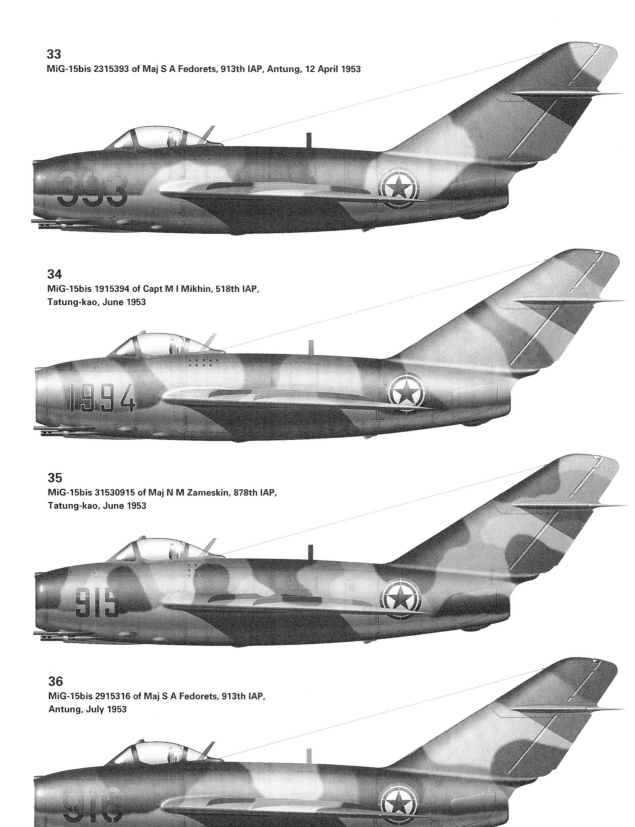

33
MiG-15bis 2315393 of Maj S A Fedorets, 913th IAP, Antung, 12 April 1953

34
MiG-15bis 1915394 of Capt M I Mikhin, 518th IAP,
Tatung-kao, June 1953

35
MiG-15bis 31530915 of Maj N M Zameskin, 878th IAP,
Tatung-kao, June 1953

36
MiG-15bis 2915316 of Maj S A Fedorets, 913th IAP,
Antung, July 1953

JANUARY – JULY 1952

The rapid build-up of the F-86 force in December 1951 created another problem for 64th IAK in the New Year – combat fatigue. MiG pilots in-theatre had been complaining about their increasing mission tempo since the summer and early autumn of 1951, and in January things got a lot worse when a number of experienced pilots (element leaders and above) were killed or badly wounded in combat. These pilots were flying more often than others in the corps, and there was evidence to suggest that their increased levels of fatigue as a result of this feverish sortie tempo was leading to a lack of alertness and a rise in the loss rate amongst 64th IAK units.

The first of the aces lost in January 1952 was 18th GvIAP flight leader Snr Lt V I Stepanov (five victories in Korea), who, on the 6th, had his MiG-15 badly shot up by an F-86 during a fierce dogfight. On landing back at his base, Stepanov's crippled fighter suffered total brake failure and ran off the end of the runway at high speed. The jet hit a bank on the airfield perimeter and burst into flames, killing the pilot.

The following day the deputy commander of 196th IAP, Capt Boris Abakumov (five Korean War victories), was forced to eject from his fighter after being shot up by a Sabre. Unfortunately, a burst of fire had shot the fingers off his left hand and fractured his left forearm. Although Abakumov recovered, his wounds kept him permanently grounded.

On 11 January 18th GvIAP flight leader Capt Lev Chukin (15 victories in Korea) was shot down in a surprise F-86 attack. The ace ejected, but he came down in rocky ground and injured his back. Once again, although Chukin recovered, he did not again fly in Korea.

Guards Capt Sergey Kramarenko was yet another veteran MiG ace forced to eject from his fighter in January 1952, the 176th GvIAP squadron leader taking to his parachute on the 17th. Forty years later, HSU winner Kramarenko remembered;

'I had just shot a Sabre down (although the USAF lists no F-86 losses on this date) when my aircraft was attacked by another American fighter. The MiG went into a spin that I couldn't recover from. I pushed the ejection lever at once and flew out. Hanging from my parachute, I saw the Sabre that had shot me down turn round and head straight for me. The pilot opened fire and tracer streaked past below me – I remember drawing up my legs. He turned round again and made a second run. There were clouds just below me, and I wondered if I could reach them before the American opened fire again. But as soon as he did I went into the cloud. It was wet and dark, but nobody could see me, and I wanted to hang there for as long as possible.

'When I came out of the cloud and looked around, I couldn't see the F-86. I looked down and saw mountain tops about 1000 m below. Then

Capt Boris Abakumov (five Korean War victories) of 196th IAP, 324th IAD ejected from his jet after being shot up by a Sabre on 7 January 1952. Badly wounded prior to taking to his parachute, Abakumov would never pilot a jet fighter again

I noticed there were trees on the mountains, and I was worried that I might get caught up in them. I spotted a clearing in the trees just before I hit the ground and somersaulted five or six times down the slope. When I finally came to a halt, I was horrified to see a large rock just ten metres away from my current position. I wondered what would have happened if I'd landed on it.

'I started examining myself. The enemy had fired at me and I thought he had hit me, although I couldn't find any bullet wounds – there was no blood anywhere, not on my hands, head or legs. My head hurt, however, and I am sure that I must have hit it either when I landed or ejected from my fighter. Happy that I was still in one piece, I gathered up my parachute and clambered down the mountain slope.

'I eventually reached a road and started walking along it, making sure that I kept the sun on my left. I walked towards the sea. Then I heard a noise and saw an old Korean riding in a cart drawn by a donkey. I quickly explained to him that I was on his side, and had indeed been defending him. We had been taught some Korean, and I told him that I was a Soviet pilot. However, it soon became clear to me that he couldn't understand a word I was saying. Perhaps my pronunciation was wrong. Eventually I was able to make my meaning clear. "Moscow – kho", meaning "well". He understood "Moscow kho" "Kho!" "Pyongyang kho?" "Kho!" "Stalin kho?" "Kho!" "Kim Il Sung kho?" "Kho!" Realising at last that I was a friend, he seated me in his cart and took me to his village.

'The Korean police were already there when we arrived, and they began checking me over. A policeman brought maps of Moscow and Korea. I showed them where I had fought against the Americans and had in turn been shot down. Finally, they found me a car to take me back to my regiment.'

64th IAK had officially lost 11 MiGs in January, which was double the number downed in the previous month. Four pilots had also been killed. These losses were the worst suffered by the Soviet fighter units since they had started flying combat missions in Korea – USAF F-86 pilots claimed 32 MiGs destroyed. Despite these losses, Corps' pilots had been credited with the destruction of 45 F-86s and two F-84s, resulting in the creation of five new aces. These successes were the last claimed by pilots from 303rd and 324th IADs, as in the second half of January they had begun handing over their aircraft to 97th and 190th IADs.

On 30 January, at 1617 hrs, a group of six MiGs from 196th IAP, led by Maj Aleksey Mitusov (seven Korean War victories), together with eight jets from newly-arrived 148th GvIAP, took off to intercept the enemy on what proved to be 324th IAD's last combat sortie in Korea. The following day, the division's pilots returned to the Soviet Union. 303rd IAD continued flying missions until mid-February, when the division handed its jets over to 190th IAD.

PAINT TRIALS

Just prior to its departure, 17th IAP had been given the task of testing different paint schemes applied to the regiment's MiGs-15bis. These had been introduced following complaints by pilots that the clear varnish factory finish that had been the norm in Korea since late 1950 made the aircraft visible from distances of up to 40-50 km (25-30 miles).

Trials with camouflaged jets had actually started in early 1951, but the advanced paint finishes devised had not meet with the approval of operational pilots. After months of rethinking the whole idea, senior officers in 64th IAK eventually asked frontline pilots to evaluate no fewer than 20 different schemes. These tests were conducted by a flight from 17th IAP that was led by Capt Nikolai Dokashenko (nine Korean War victories). The pilots involved were Dokashenko himself, Capts N S Volkov (seven victories in Korea) and V Khvostantsev (four victories) and Snr Lt A Nikolaev (four victories).

The end result of these trials was the adoption of a scheme that had the jet's uppersurfaces painted in silver-green overall and the underside in mid blue. MiGs of 64th IAK started receiving the new finish in February.

During that same month 303rd IAD pilots scored six more victories and lost one aircraft prior to them leaving Tatung-kao on the 20th.

Between November 1950 and January 1951, the pilots of 64th IAK had flown 18,759 day and 344 night combat sorties. Some 307 day and 16 night aerial engagements had been fought during the course of these missions. All told, corps pilots had been credited with the destruction of 564 enemy aircraft – 48 B-29s, three B-26s, two RB-45s, two 'F-47s', 20 F-51s, 103 F-80s, 132 F-84s, 218 F-86s, eight 'F-94s', 25 Meteor F 8s and three 'F6F-5s'. The 'F-47s' were almost certainly Skyraiders, the 'F-94s' more likely to have been F9F Panthers and the 'F6F-5s' were probably F4U Corsairs. In return, the corps had lost 71 MiGs-15s and MiG-15bis, resulting in the deaths of 34 pilots.

Some 41 pilots of 50th, 303rd and 324th IADs and 151st GvIAD had scored five or more victories in Korea, and 19 of them received the highly coveted title of Hero of the Soviet Union. The latter were Maj Stepan Bakhaev, Capt Grigoriy Ges, Capt Nikolai Dokashenko, Capt Sergey Kramarenko, Maj Georgiy Lobov, Capt Stepan Naumenko, Maj Boris Obraztsov, Maj Dmitri Oskin, Capt Grigoriy Okhay, Col Evgeniy Pepelyaev, Maj Mikhail Ponomarev, Lt Col Grigoriy Pulov, Snr Lt Dmitriy Samoylov, Lt Col Aleksander Smorchkov, Capt Evgeniy Stelmakh, Maj Serafim Subbotin, Maj Nikolay Sutyagin, Snr Lt Fedor Shebanov and Capt Lev Shchukin.

NEW DIVISIONS ARRIVE

On 15 December 1951, MiG-15bis-equipped 97th IAD, which had been defending the southwest approaches to Moscow, was ordered by Soviet Defence Minister Marshal Vasilevskiy to join 64th IAK. Fellow MiG-15bis regiment 190th IAD was also assigned to the corps at the same time, these units replacing the by now battle-weary 303rd and 324th IADs in Manchuria.

Pilots of Capt Nikolai Dokashenko's flight in 17th IAP, 303rd IAD. They are, from left to right, Capt Nikolai Volkov (seven Korean War victories), Snr Lt Aleksey Nikolaev (four victories), Capt Vladimir Khvostantsev (four victories), and Capt Nikolai Dokashenko (nine victories)

Twelve-kill ace Lt Col Aleksander Smorchkov (deputy CO of the 18th GvIAP) and 15-kill ace Capt Lev Shchukin (18th GvIAP flight leader) were photographed at Tatung-kao in January 1952

Only the flight personnel and commanding officers of the 97th IAD's 16th IAP, 148th GvIAP and the divisional headquarters would ultimately be committed to the Korean conflict. Crossing the Soviet-Chinese border on 1 January 1952, they arrived in Antung the following day. By the middle of the month, 97th IAD had accepted aircraft and groundcrews from 324th IAD, and on the 25th divisional pilots began flying combat sorties against small groups of US aircraft.

190th IAD (consisting of 17th, 494th and 821st IAPs) was deployed to Primorie, in eastern USSR, in early 1950. When 17th IAP was attached to 303rd IAD in October of that year, 256th IAP was formed to take its place. 190th IAD left its aircraft at Primorie and arrived at Tatung-kao to replace 303rd IAD on 20 January 1952. On receiving its MiGs from the latter division, 190th IAD went straight into action, with the first significant clash taking place on 14 February when its pilots intercepted small groups of Sabres. Six days later 190th IAD attempted to repulse a series of massive air strikes.

Unfortunately, the start to combat operations made by 97th and 190th IADs was not overly successful. In February, 64th IAK was credited with shooting down 16 F-86s, but lost 11 MiGs and six pilots, and had a further 19 jets damaged – the USAF acknowledged the loss of just two Sabres to MiGs, claiming 17 Soviet fighters destroyed in return. Six of the 16 victories had been scored by the now highly experienced pilots of the departing 303rd IAD, which lost just one MiG-15bis, while the new arrivals posted a similar number of victories and losses. Despite the customary inflation of the victory tally, it is clear that the February clashes had, in the main, gone against 97th and 190th IADs. There were two reasons for this.

The first was the considerably more complex combat environment that now existed in Korea. The strength of the Sabre units tasked with performing fighter sweeps had increased significantly in February, which in turn meant that the area they now covered was some 150 km (94 miles) deep. Elements of F-86s patrolling the skies from Sukchon up to Antung provided US fighter-bombers with reliable protection against the MiGs. When scrambled to intercept enemy attack aircraft, the Soviet units simply got caught up in the pack of fighters. It is not by chance that only one out of the 58 aerial engagements in February was fought between MiGs and F-84s, while the rest were battles with Sabres.

Soviet fighters had to start fighting in smaller groups – flights and squadrons – but the new pilots brought in to replace those from 303rd and 324th IADs lacked the required skills to deal with their opponents flying F-86s. And therein lay the second reason for the lack of success.

Flight and squadron leaders were now reluctant to split their pilots up into small, manoeuvrable teams of two or four jets, instead choosing to stick together and operate as complete groups. Pairs of aircraft as well as individual pilots would now often lag behind their group formations after the latter were bounced by the marauding Sabres, who continued to sortie in two- and four-ship flights.

There was also a lack of caution within the new regiments in-theatre because their aircrew had little experience in high-speed, high-altitude fighter operations. As a result, pilots were now paying too much attention to simply flying their aircraft, and not enough on keeping a watch out for the enemy. This in turn meant that it was impossible for 64th IAK to send pilots out to fight UN fighter-bombers at low altitudes because such operations required polished flying skills, good teamwork among pairs and flights, the precise employment of combat tactics and keen situational awareness.

Things got even worse for the Soviet MiG pilots in March, when the Sabre wings concentrated on securing air superiority in areas near to 64th IAK's bases. This offensive saw F-86s wheeling over the Yalu estuary and regularly intruding into Chinese airspace – something that had rarely happened in the past. Enemy fighter-bombers also changed tactics, switching from large-scale air operations involving a massive number of jets to a constant series of sorties flown by small groups over several hours.

If Soviet MiGs appeared, the US fighter-bombers flew back across the coastline and circled over Korea Bay while they waited for the communist jets to leave. 64th IAK simply did not have enough aircraft and pilots to fly continuous MiG patrols in the American fighter-bombers' area of operations, which meant that UN attack aircraft were able to deliver air strikes against areas north of Anju for the first time since September 1951.

Yet the MiGs still posed a clear threat to the F-80s and F-84s in particular, and these types would usually only risk operating north of Chonju and over the Yalu River in adverse weather. They immediately made a run for it at the first sight of the MiGs, however.

With more UN aircraft now operating in North Korean skies that ever before, the intensity of combat sorties flown by 64th IAK continued to increase. In March, Soviet fighters participated in 89 group air engagements, which was one-and-a-half times more than had been fought in February. As in the previous month, there was only one clash with enemy fighter-bombers, but it was a successful one, and it enabled two future aces to open their combat scores. One was HSU and commander of 821st IAP, Maj Grigoriy Dmitryuk, who had flown 206 combat sorties, fought in 37 air engagements and scored 18 kills in World War 2 – he would add five more over Korea, becoming 64th IAK's 46th ace on 11 July 1952. The other pilot was Dmitryuk's deputy, Maj Afanasiy Olenitsa, who would also score five Korean War victories. Dmitryuk and Olenitsa each claimed an F-80.

Capt Vladimir Zabelin (nine Korean War victories) of 821st IAP, who was to be the highest-scoring pilot of 64th IAK in 1952-53, opened his account on 16 March when he engaged a Sabre from a range of 300 m (325 yrd). The F-86 tried to do a wing-over and break off the engagement, but Zabelin managed to stay on the fighter's tail and keep it in his sights. He manoeuvred rapidly to close the range, continually firing at the F-86. After his second burst the Sabre started smoking and dived steeply. Zabelin assumed his fire had damaged the enemy fighter's engine, as he reported seeing it spin into the ground (the USAF list no Sabres lost on this date, however).

Fellow future ace Capt Anatoliy Bashman (five Korean War victories) of 148th GvIAP claimed his first kill five days later (again no losses reported by the USAF), while Dmitryuk and Olenitsa scored again on the 24th – the 4th FW lost a single F-86A to a MiG on this date.

Snr Lt Omelchenko was shot down during the first dogfight of the 24th, but he managed to eject safely (USAF Sabres claimed three kills).

Olenitsa covered him as he hung in his parachute, and when one of the Sabre pilots tried to machine gun Omelchenko, Olenitsa hit it with several well aimed bursts. The F-86 started smoking, dived steeply and was deemed to have been shot down – a 4th FW jet returned to base badly shot up.

Maj Dmitryuk got his kill during the second engagement of the day, when he and his wingman took on a pair of F-86s in a vertical dogfight. Closing to within 500 m (540 yrd) of the trailing F-86, Dmitryuk opened fire. His rounds hit home, and he followed his initial salvo up with four more bursts that started a fire in the Sabre's rear fuselage. The MiG pilot saw his opponent slide open his canopy and eject.

This F-86 was one of 47 enemy aircraft that the pilots of 97th and 190th IADs were credited with having shot down in March 1952. This figure comprised 43 F-86s and four F-80s, although few of these kills can be matched up with losses officially published by USAF units. 64th IAK lost 16 MiGs and four pilots, and had a further 43 aircraft damaged, during the same period. Sabre pilots claimed 39 MiG kills in March.

April brought more difficulties, with US pilots seemingly disregarding the North Korean-Chinese border (despite the UN mandate forbidding them from flying over Chinese territory) altogether and actively operating over Antung and Tatung-kao. Soviet MiGs were now being routinely attacked as they took off and landed at these bases. Later in the month USAF Sabres shifted from attacking individual Soviet aircraft to blockading 64th IAK airfields.

In April the corps lost 18 MiG-15bis fighters and six pilots, with an additional 32 jets being damaged. Nine of the aircraft destroyed had been downed while taking off or landing. USAF Sabre pilots were credited with downing 44 MiGs and destroying two more communist jet fighters on the ground.

Yet despite these losses, some Soviet aviators managed to shoot down Sabres as they patrolled over the MiG bases. Nine-kill ace Maj V M Zabelin of 821st IAP was one such pilot. Returning from a dogfight on 2 April, he saw an F-86 attacking a MiG-15 on final approach with its landing gear extended. Zabelin fired at the Sabre, which started smoking and banked towards Korea Bay. The 51st FW F-86E crashed near Dadonggang at 1710 hrs.

Over the next ten days Vladimir Zabelin claimed two more victories, Maj Olenitsa downed one enemy aircraft and Anatoliy Bashman took his tally to five.

On the 13th, Zabelin became the first of the new 64th IAK intake to reach five victories when he downed another F-86E from the 51st FW. Capt Arkadiy Boytsov, deputy squadron leader from 16th IAP, also opened his account that same day. The Sabre he attacked burst into flames and headed for the sea trailing a plume of white smoke. Boytsov was unable to finish it off prior to turning back for the coast, however (the USAF lists only a solitary F-86 loss on this date).

Grigoriy Dmitryuk scored another victory on the 18th, firing three bursts from all of his guns at a Sabre while it was making a turn. Two 37 mm shells hit the jet's port wing and the F-86 exploded – the pilot was not seen to eject from his stricken fighter (no Sabre loss was recorded by the USAF on this date).

Following a month of clashing with a seemingly endless stream of Sabre formations, a small group of 64th IAK pilots finally got amongst USAF fighter-bombers on 30 April, as Capt Boytsov recalled;

'The Commander of Air Defence Fighter Aviation, Savitskiy, who headed a team of senior Air Force and Air Defence Force officers tasked with studying combat experience in North Korea, arrived at Antung on the morning of 30 April, together with Maj Gen Lobov, 64th IAK CO. Savitskiy told pilots "You will no longer operate in regimental-size groups. It's high time you stopped fighting like that!" Lobov ordered us to "Go on a free hunt in flights, maintaining radio silence. We'll guide you to the target from the ground with the help of radar. In case of emergency, you'll be pulled back".'

The 64th IAK commander ordered five flights to take off. Only the group from 16th IAP, led by Capt Petr Minervin (three Korean War victories), managed to intercept the USAF fighter-bombers – F-80Cs from the 8th FBG. Capt Boytsov was part of this flight;

'Six of us took off in a group – Minervin and Morshchikhin, Tokarev and Levin, and I was paired up with Tolubenskiy. We were flying with external fuel tanks at an altitude of 10,000 m (32,500 ft). When we passed Anju, we were told by our ground controller to "Turn to starboard – there's a group of US aircraft ahead". I had just started the turn when I saw three groups of four enemy attack aircraft. We dropped our external fuel tanks and went after them.'

Each pair of Soviet fighters selected its own flight of F-80s to attack, with Minervin managing to set a Shooting Star on fire in his first pass – its pilot ejected. By the time Minervin had started his second attack, the enemy fighter-bombers had already formed a defensive circle. This failed to stop the MiG pilot from setting another F-80 alight after firing at it from a distance of 300 m.

The US aircraft were also being fired at from the ground by local flak batteries throughout this engagement, their barrage being so heavy that the MiGs lost their formation integrity during the clash.

Anti-aircraft fire did little to unsettle Maj Tokarev, however, and he too claimed two victories. Shortly after scoring his second kill, Tokarev and his wingman watched an F-80 that was being chased by a MiG crash into a hill. Capt Boytsov also increased his score by downing a Shooting Star (its pilot was also seen to bail out). Turning to starboard after despatching the jet, Arkadiy Boytsov immediately spotted another flight of F-80s ahead of him. Closing in to 300-400 m, he opened fire. One of the Shooting Stars soon started emitting black smoke and began to descend towards the sea. Boytsov subsequently reported;

'We attacked the enemy fighter-bombers while they were dropping their ordnance, but we started running out of fuel because we were flying at low level. We headed for our home base, although my wingman and I didn't have enough fuel to reach the airfield so we landed at Sinuiju to top up our tanks. We flew back to Antung that same evening. All of us were decorated after this dogfight – everyone got the Order of the Red Banner, and I received the Order of Lenin. We were all promoted as well, captains to majors and senior lieutenants to captains.'

Initially, the Soviet pilots were credited with downing five enemy aircraft, but the wreckage of the one that Tokarev and Levin had watched

Capt Petr Minervin (three Korean War victories) was deputy squadron leader of 16th IAP, 97th IAD

crash was found later, and it was reportedly a Thunderjet – Arkadiy Boytsov was credited with the kill. No F-84s were lost in Korea on this date, although three F-80Cs were listed as lost in action by the USAF.

All told, Soviet pilots were credited with downing 52 enemy aircraft in April 1952, including 44 F-86s, three F-84s, four F-80s and an F-51. Again, very few of these victories tally with USAF losses, with the Sabre wings losing just three jets to MiGs according to their records.

REVISED TACTICS

Buoyed by the success of 30 April, 64th IAK ordered all regiments to operate primarily in small groups during May. Indeed, more than 80 per cent of all combat sorties flown were undertaken by elements in squadron or flight size. Such tactics yielded results, with 20 of the 57 air engagements fought during the month seeing MiGs attacking enemy fighter-bombers. The aerial successes enjoyed by the Soviet pilots were quite impressive, with a total of 33 daytime kills being credited to the MiG regiments. Of this figure, 20 aircraft – seven F-84s, five F-80s, seven F-51s and an F4U-4 – were attack aircraft. An RB-26C was also shot down by Snr Lt Kurganov of 351st IAP on the night of 15 May (confirmed by the USAF).

These victories were scored at the cost of 16 MiGs destroyed and four pilots killed, with 14 more jets damaged. As in April, half the Soviet fighters lost were shot down either during take-off or landing. Sabre pilots claimed 32 MiGs shot down and five destroyed on the ground.

To counter the enemy's crippling blockade of the airfields at Antung and Tatung-kao, Air Defence Fighter Aviation decided to redeploy two MiG regiments to second-line bases outside the Sabres' range in early May. Such a move would now give the Soviet command the opportunity to scramble aircraft in an attempt to lift the blockade on airfields outside the Antung complex.

494th IAP left for Anshan on 5 May and 16th IAP redeployed to Mukden-West airfield on the 13th. In turn, 351st IAP and a nightfighter unit from 133rd IAD were sent to Antung from Anshan and Mukden-West 48 hours later. On 16 May, a 351st IAP squadron that had been training on MiG-15bis fighters since February redeployed from Anshan.

133rd IAD, comprising 147th GvIAP and 415th and 726th IAPs, had joined 64th IAK in-theatre from the Soviet Union in mid-April. Its regiments, deployed at Mukden-West and Dongfeng, immediately started training for combat operations in North Korea. As mentioned in the previous paragraph, a MiG-15-equipped nightfighter squadron from 147th GvIAP completed its training in mid-May and was sent to Antung on the 15th of that month. The arrival of this unit in-theatre significantly boosted the strength of the Soviet nightfighter force committed to the war, but the hard-pressed day fighter regiments received no such reinforcement.

By mid-May, 97th and 190th IADs had just 92 combat-capable pilots on strength – the official pre-war establishment strength was 154 pilots. And when two regiments were redeployed to the rear several days later, both divisions were left with just 60 frontline pilots in Antung and Tatung-kao. Nevertheless, on 17 May 190th IAD fought one of the most successful battles with enemy fighter-bombers in 64th IAK's history.

Seen at Tatung-kao airfield in February 1952, Viktor Kolmanson (one Korean War victory), who was 256th IAP, 190th IAD navigation officer, provides a light for 11-kill ace Grigoriy Okhay of 523rd IAP, 303rd IAD. Kolmanson was shot down and killed while landing on 20 May 1952

Shortly after dawn, Soviet radars detected 64 enemy aircraft flying in a northwesterly direction, and 16 MiGs from 494th and 821st IAPs were scrambled to intercept them. Six 494th IAP jets duly engaged Thunderjets from the 49th FBG and 136th FBW at 0610 hrs. Eight minutes later fighters from the 821st IAP also made contact with the USAF fighter-bombers, Vladimir Zabelin, who was now a major, leading his wingman in to attack a flight of four Thunderjets. Dropping behind the last F-84 in the formation, he fired a long burst from 270 m (300 yrd) that tore the jet's port wing off. The Thunderjet plunged vertically into a hill and exploded.

Zabelin then went in pursuit of two more F-84s, but he could not overhaul them before they had fled south over the Korean coastline.

Soviet pilots were credited with a total of six kills following this engagement, Lt Col Olenitsa downing two Thunderjets to take his tally to five. 821st IAP CO Lt Col Dmitryuk also shot down an F-84. The USAF confirmed the loss of four Thunderjets.

After the losses of 17 May, USAF fighter-bomber units changed their tactics. They now approached targets at low level from the direction of Korea Bay, thus preventing Soviet radar from detecting them in advance of their arrival. 64th IAK's shortage of assets also had a progressively negative effect on the corps' ability to counter UN air strikes as the month wore on. The MiGs could only be scrambled to intercept a few of the many groups of enemy fighters and fighter-bombers that were now regularly attacking targets in the north on a daily basis. Yet the Soviet pilots kept inflicting losses on the enemy formations.

Maj Vladimir Zabelin downed 4th FW Sabres on 20 and 21 May (both confirmed by USAF records), the latter aircraft being caught prowling over the Soviet airfields near Antung and Tatung-kao. Returning from a combat mission, Zabelin and his wingman had initially been bounced by four Sabres. In order to shake them off their tails, the two Soviet pilots started climbing, but when they broke through the clouds above them they were attacked by another flight of F-86s. Zabelin quickly led his wingman back into the clouds, this time heading earthward. When he reached the cloud base, the ace spotted a pair of Sabres right in front of him. Firing a long burst at one of them from 370 m (400 yrd), Zabelin succeeded in sending the trailing jet down northwest of Phihen.

Soviet MiGs encountered USAF Mustangs for the last time on 31 May when a flight of four jets from 148th GvIAP, led by Maj Bashman, intercepted an identical number of F/RF-51Ds from the 18th FBG. In the ensuing engagement, the Soviet pilots were credited with four kills, although only a single Mustang was lost. One of the victories was claimed by Anatoly Bashman, thus making him 64th IAK's 44th ace.

Bad weather restricted flying in June, when Soviet fighter pilots fought just 19 daytime engagements, compared with 57 in May. The June battles were anything but successful, with only two Sabres and three Thunderjets being downed at a cost of eight MiGs and one pilot – five more Soviet aircraft sustained damage (the USAF credited its Sabre pilots with 18 MiG kills). These losses were attributable to a combination of battle fatigue and insufficient strength, as the number of mission-capable 97th and 190th IAD pilots in-theatre dropped by 12 during the course of the month.

Apart from its nightfighter squadron, 133rd IAD had not yet been committed to combat because its regiments were still being trained up. This meant that the remaining MiG units in-theatre were tasked with intercepting UN attack aircraft without having the numbers necessary to counter the enemy fighter sweeps and escorts for the fighter-bombers. Sabre units also continued to routinely prowl around the MiG bases in considerable numbers.

The USAF exploited this situation to the full on 23 June when it targeted the Suphun hydroelectric power plant – one of the key facilities protected by 64th IAK. The Soviet fighters were unable to blunt the attack, as 20 Sabres effectively blockaded the corps' airfields. Forty more F-86s flew a fighter sweep ahead of the fighter-bombers, with a similar number providing the latter with close escort. Finally, MiGs based further afield at Mukden and Anshan could not be scrambled to lift the Sabre threat to the Soviet airfields because of bad weather. And without the support of these aircraft, attempting to launch MiGs from Antung and Tatung-kao would have resulted in huge and pointless losses at the hands of the blockading F-86s. As a result, no Soviet fighters took off to counter the strike.

NIGHTFIGHTER SUCCESSES

If 64th IAK was not particularly successful in daytime operations during this period, Soviet nightfighters were able to revive memories of the October 1951 'Black Week' for FEAF Bomber Command. The leader of 351st IAP's Lavochkin fighter squadron, Capt Dushin, opened the June account on the night of 5th when he shot down a B-26C of the 3rd BG, which crashed in flames into the sea 10-15 km (6-9 miles) southeast of Sinmi-do Island. It was, however, to be the last enemy aircraft to be downed by 64th IAK's La-11 pilots. The official results of their nine months of combat operations were five B-26s destroyed and one B-26 and two B-29s damaged.

Now operating almost exclusively at night, 19th BG Superfortresses attacked railway bridges near Pakchon on 10-11 June. Four MiG-15s were scrambled to intercept them, their pilots, 147th GvIAP CO Lt Col Studilin, his deputy Maj Bykovets, 351st IAP navigation officer Capt Anatoliy Karelin and Snr Lt Ikhsangaliev, being ordered to defend targets in the Antung area. Studilin was the first to encounter the enemy. He attacked an illuminated B-29, which dived steeply and banked away towards the sea.

Anatoliy Karelin, who was to be 64th IAK's only nightfighter ace, and the highest-scoring nightfighter pilot of the Korean War with six kills, was next into action. He performed a head-on attack on a B-29 illuminated by searchlights,

Future six-kill nightfighter ace Capt A M Karelin of 351st IAP climbs down from the cockpit of his MiG-15bis at Antung in the autumn of 1951. Standing in the foreground is Maj Kultyshev (one Korean War victory)

opening fire from a distance of 300-400 m. The bomber exploded and debris fell to the ground 15-20 km southeast of Sonchon. While Karelin was recovering from this attack, his MiG was damaged by wreckage from the B-29, which pierced and dented his port wing and badly scratched his canopy.

Six minutes into the engagement Anatoliy Karelin saw a second Superfortress, again illuminated by a searchlight, and fired a single burst at it from behind. The B-29 caught fire, dropped its bombs in haste and headed for the sea, descending rapidly. Knowing that the coast was only several miles away, Karelin did not chase the retreating Superfortress.

Continuing with his patrol, he saw yet another illuminated bomber 20 minutes later. Firing a long burst from a distance of 300-400 m whilst immediately behind his target, Karelin watched the B-29 head for the sea trailing flames. Quickly losing altitude, the bomber eventually crashed into the water 35 km (22 miles) from the coast. Karelin saw PT boats approaching the scene to search for the downed bomber's crew. The 64th IAK command-and-control post also observed both of Karelin's victims go down, and their loss was confirmed by the USAF. These aircraft were the first B-29s to be shot down by 64th IAK nightfighter pilots, but they were certainly not the last.

At 2135 hrs on 15 June, Snr Lt Volodarskiy of 147th GvIAP intercepted an illuminated B-29 ten kilometres (six miles) west of Chonju. After four attacks, the pilot reported that the Superfortress crashed into the sea 10-15 km west of Cape Hanchen (no such loss was recorded by the USAF).

Anatoliy Karelin enjoyed more success on the night of 3/4 July when he was ordered to the Anju area. At 2246 hrs he spotted RB-29A 44-61727 from the 91st Strategic Reconnaissance Squadron (SRS) framed in a searchlight beam. Karelin set the aircraft on fire in his first attack, and subsequently made three more passes using the flames billowing from the aircraft's wing centre section as an aiming point. At an altitude of about 2000 m (6500 ft), the RB-29A started breaking up, and the bulk of

MiG-15bis 53201546 of 351st IAP is readied for a night combat sortie at Antung in 1952

Maj Vladimir Fedorets of 726th IAP, 133rd IAD scored two Korean War victories

the wreckage hit the ground and exploded two kilometres west of Pakchon. One crewman was killed, one posted missing in action and eleven were captured.

In contrast to the successes of the nightfighter pilots, early July proved to be a lean time for the corps' day fighter pilots. In fact, 64th IAK suffered its heaviest losses of the Korean War on 4 July when it had no fewer than 11 MiGs shot down and one pilot killed (the USAF credited its Sabre pilots with 13 MiG kills). 494th IAP bore the brunt of these losses, losing seven MiG-15s. The regiment had been scrambled to counter an enemy fighter sweep, but soon after take-off, it was ordered to intercept Thunderjets that had unexpectedly appeared nearby. 494th IAP now faced a numerically superior enemy force in a tactically unfavourable situation, and it paid the price. 64th IAK did not lose any more aircraft or pilots during the rest of July, however (F-86 pilots claimed four more MiGs destroyed later that month).

Hoping to relieve the pressure on the Antung and Tatung-kao-based units that were now effectively under siege from the air, 64th IAK hastily opened a new airfield at Dapu in late June and immediately transferred 256th IAP in from Anshan on the 30th. 726th IAP, 133rd IAD, joined the regiment at Dapu on 12 July. Earlier that same month, on the 7th and 9th, 133rd's 147th and 415th IAPs redeployed to Antung, while 148th GvIAP joined 16th IAP at Mukden-West.

July had also seen pilots from 97th and 190th IADs score their last victories, while those from 133rd IAD opened their Korean War accounts. Maj Arkadiy Boytsov of 97th IAD destroyed a lone F-86E from the 51st FG over Fynchen on 12 July for his sixth, and last, kill. He opened fire at a range of 350 m (380 yrd) and hit the Sabre's starboard wing, causing the F-86E to break up prior to hitting the ground. Boytsov was recommended for the coveted title of Hero of the Soviet Union following this kill, but he did not receive the award until 14 July 1953.

133rd IAD claimed its first daytime victories on 16 July when 726th IAP engaged F-86Es from the 51st FW 15 km northeast of Antung. Maj Degtyarev (three Korean War victories), who was leading the MiGs, attacked a pair of Sabres but missed his target. The enemy fighters were then attacked by Maj Vladimir Fedorets (two Korean War victories), who succeeded in hitting one with several cannon rounds just as the F-86s attempted to bank away. The USAF fighter exploded in mid-air, and its loss was confirmed by the 51st FW.

821st IAP ranking ace Maj Vladimir Zabelin downed his ninth, and last, enemy aircraft over North Korea on 20 July when eight MiG-15s took on 34 F-86s from the 4th FW. Singling out a Sabre, Zabelin stuck to its tail despite his opponent doing his level best to shake him off. Closing in to 400 m (430 yrd), Zabelin fired a long burst, after which the F-86 levelled off and decelerated sharply. When the range halved, Zabelin again opened fire, setting the Sabre ablaze and forcing its pilot to eject (the loss was confirmed by the 4th FW).

Although 190th and 97th IADs remained assigned to 64th IAK until the middle and the end of August, respectively, they no longer participated in active combat operations, for they had started to hand over their aircraft to their replacement divisions (32nd and 216th IADs) from late July.

AUGUST – DECEMBER 1952

As mentioned at the end of the previous chapter, July-August 1952 saw a comprehensive change in the MiG-15 units assigned to 64th IAK in Manchuria. 216th IAD was the first of the new divisions to arrive in-theatre, its trio of regiments replacing 190th IAD's constituent units in late July (the latter were then posted to northeastern China, before returning to the USSR). 216th IAD's 518th and 878th IAPs were initially based at Tatung-kao, with 676th IAP operating from nearby Dapu.

In August, 32nd IAD, having relieved 97th IAD, took up residence at Mukden-West. Its trio of regiments (224th, 525th and 913th IAPs) flew from Anshan, however.

The newly arrived pilots, operating alongside their brethren from 133rd IAD, who had been in-theatre since mid-May 1952, were charged with gaining air supremacy overhead their own airfields and intercepting enemy fighter-bombers. 133rd and 216th IADs would operate from frontline airfields, with the former countering low-level attacks and the latter taking on the Sabres at high altitude. The 32nd IAD was to cover the Antung airfield complex in an attempt to make it safe for MiGs to operate from there.

On 19 August, after several weeks of operational area study, division flight commander, and future ranking ace, Snr Lt Mikhail Mikhin (nine Korean War kills) gained his first victory. Spotting a pair of Sabres, he and his wingman attacked them. The American pilots tried to avoid their pursuers by making a tight right-hand turn, but Mikhin managed to fire a burst at the trailing F-86. His first rounds passed behind the target, so Mikhin increased the lead and fired a long burst from 200 m (220 yrd). A tracer round hit the Sabre, but due to the high closure rate the MiG pilot did not see the result of his attack. As Mikhin turned to avoid hitting the US fighter, Snr Lt Yakovlev observed the F-86 dive away smoking (no losses were reported by the USAF on this date).

In August MiG pilots were credited with 17 victories, 16 of them being Sabres and the 17th a Thunderjet (three F-86s and one F-84 were lost to MiGs according to USAF records). The sole fighter-bomber – an F-84E from the 58th FBG – was downed on 6 August over the Sunchon area by two MiGs from 726th IAP. 64th IAK losses for the month totalled 18 MiGs-15bis and seven pilots, with a further 19 jets damaged (33 MiGs were claimed by F-86 pilots, with two more being credited to Royal Navy Sea Fury unit 802 Naval Air Squadron).

In September the Sabres stepped up their aggressive sweeps of the Soviet bases in Antung, resulting in no fewer than 41 MiGs-15bis being shot down and 13 pilots killed. Almost half – 19 aircraft – were downed over 64th IAK's own airfields. The loss rate amongst pilots during

Capt Mikhail Mikhin, photographed here in September 1952, claimed nine victories, making him 518th IAP's sole Korean War ace

Maj Konstantin Degtyarev scored three Korean War victories while serving as a squadron leader with 726th IAP. Subsequently promoted to lieutenant colonel, he was commanding 147th GvIAP by war's end

A photograph of the wrecked F-86 shot down by Capt Mikhin on 9 September 1952. USAF sources list no Sabres losses due to combat on that day, although an F-86A from the 4th FW crashed when its engine flamed out. Three F-84Es fell victim to MiGs on the 9th, however

take-offs and landings exceeded 60 per cent, and aviators ejecting from low altitude had no chance of survival, as they lacked sufficient height to allow their parachutes to open properly. USAF Sabre units claimed 64 MiG kills and Marine Corps FG-1D Corsair pilot Capt Jesse Folmar was credited with a solitary MiG victory just prior to being shot down by a second communist jet.

Despite suffering unprecedented losses, 64th IAK pilots still managed to inflict a series of major blows on UN fighter-bomber formations in September. The divisions claimed 40 Sabres, 18 Thunderjets and an FG-1D shot down – USAF losses to MiGs amounted to eight F-86s and four F-84s, and the Marine Corps recorded the loss of an FG-1D. Four of the Sabres destroyed were downed on 4 September, with one of them being claimed by Capt Mikhail Mikhin as his second F-86 kill. The future ace recalled;

'We were returning from a mission, and it was high time for us to land. As usual, we weren't returning in full strength – it was a rare thing when we did. We usually came back in pairs. Reaching the airfield, I heard a call on the radio. What was wrong? "Sabres are over the airfield! Pankov, you are under attack!" Pankov, a pilot from our regiment, turned away from the runway and raised his landing gear, but by then he had been hit. There was a flash and the aircraft fell away, at which point Pankov ejected.

'I then saw a Sabre at low altitude. Its engine was smoking heavily, making it easily visible amongst the mass of aircraft that now filled the sky. I caught up with the enemy fighter in its first turn. The aircraft was disengaging and its speed was low. I didn't have much speed either, but enough. I fired at the fuselage near the cockpit. The Sabre started smoking and dived into the bay. I didn't see where it crashed, but the pilot, who turned out to be a first lieutenant, ejected and was taken prisoner. Later, I saw him being interrogated by the Chinese.'

On 9 September 726th IAP clashed with 48 F-84s, escorted by 64 Sabres, while defending the Tagvan region of North Korea. Two groups of Soviet fighters (totalling 18 aircraft), led by regimental commander Lt Col Leonid Goryachko (two victories in Korea) and squadron commander Maj Konstantin Degtyarev (three Korean War kills), intercepted the strike at noon. Three MiGs and a pilot were lost in the engagement, but regimental pilots reported that six Thunderjets had been shot down and six more damaged – 64th IAK credited the regiment with the destruction of 14 F-84s, although the USAF acknowledged the loss of just three Thunderjets to MiGs.

133rd IAD's 147th GvIAP found itself in the thick of things on 21 September, when its pilots intercepted the first wave of attacking fighter-bombers. Having claimed three Thunderjets shot down (no losses were recorded by the USAF), the MiG pilots forced the rest of the jets to abandon their attack. One

Snr Lt Yuriy Dobrovichan of 147th GvIAP, 133rd IAD was credited with the destruction of three B-29s at night during his combat tour

A wall newspaper devoted to Snr Lt Yuriy Dobrovichan's victory over a B-29 from the 307th BG on the night of 12 September 1952

The wreckage of 307th BG B-29A 44-86343, downed by Snr Lt Yuriy Dobrovichan on the night of 12 September

week later, Capt Nikolay Zameskin, 878th IAP deputy squadron leader and the second highest-scoring 216th IAD ace (six victories in Korea), shot down his first Sabre over his own airfield (an F-86F was lost by the 4th FW on this date).

September was also a successful month for 64th IAK's nightfighter pilots, for at 2311 hrs on the 12th, Snr Lt Yuriy Dobrovichan of 147th GvIAP destroyed a 307th BG B-29 that was attacking the Suiho hydro-electric plant. Dobrovichan hit the bomber with a single burst fired from a distance of just 300 m (325 yrd). Four minutes after the attack, burning fragments of Superfortress were spotted falling into a forest 17 km (ten miles) east of Tagvan.

In October, the USAF's campaign of blockading 64th IAK bases came to an abrupt end, and the Soviet loss rate dropped accordingly – only two out of nine MiGs-15bis lost that month were shot down near an airfield. Total losses in battles with Sabres at normal combat altitudes amounted to seven aircraft and two pilots (USAF F-86 units claimed 26 MiGs destroyed).

At the same time, corps fighter pilots claimed 28 F-86s, two F4U-4s and a Meteor destroyed – the USAF admitted the loss of three Sabres to MiGs, and the US Navy also confirmed the downing of two Corsairs, but no Meteors were lost in combat. The MiG pilots had had little opportunity to engage Thunderjets in October, as they were operating south of the Chongchon River. Indeed, they only made one flight to the north during the entire month.

Capt Zameskin was amongst the MiG pilots to enjoy success in October, claiming two victories. Here, he recalls the first of these, downed on the 3rd;

'We were in a group of eight led by regimental commander Dronov, who scored three victories in Korea. The enemy had a much more

Pilots of 878th IAP are seen with the MiG-15bis 2015363 of deputy squadron leader, and six-kill ace, Capt Nikolay Zameskin at Tatung-kao during the winter of 1952/53. They are, from left to right, Zameskin's wingman Snr Lt Kashin, flight leader Capt Kaloshin, Capt Vasiliev and Capt Zameskin

Pilots of 878th IAP, 216th IAD pose for a formal photograph in early 1953. Seated are Maj Zameskin and Capt Kashin, and standing are (left) Capt Skorov (two Korean War victories) and Maj Kazakov of 518th IAP (three Korean War victories)

advantageous position, and was able to attack our first echelon. In a rapid manoeuvre, the commander half-looped in a climb. The combat formation changed, and I looked behind me to check that my wing-man was still in position. I saw nobody – my tail was exposed to enemy attack. Suddenly, I heard the familiar voice of Vladimir Voshkin, the CO's wingman, call-ing for assistance. "I'm under attack. I need help!"

'Initially, I couldn't see him. Then I spotted two aircraft, one behind the other. I made a steep turn. The aircraft was shaking, and it was difficult to keep the target under steady aim. But the sight began edging towards the cockpit and I opened fire with all three cannon. The shells hit the engine and the American aircraft began gradually turning upside down. At that moment I felt hits on my machine. I cried out to my wingman Vasya Kashin "What are you looking at? I'm under attack!" He answered, "Calm down, there's nobody there".

'By then the encounter had ended, and I had saved my comrade-in-arms. He managed to land his MiG near a rice field. There were more than 100 bullet holes in the aircraft, but it hadn't let the pilot down. Our airfield was blocked, so we landed in Anshan. In the evening, we flew back to Tatung-kao, where my maintenance crew discovered that my aircraft's air intake and intake duct had been damaged by fire from my opponent. I had brought back evidence of the battle.'

An increase in the number of MiGs in-theatre and the adoption of more robust defensive operations over Soviet airfields in Manchuria effectively put a stop to Sabre operations around 64th IAK bases in November. Just six MiGs and a single pilot were lost in daytime engagements, all during high-altitude dogfights (Sabre units claimed 29 MiGs destroyed and F9F pilots were credited with two Soviet jets). In return, 64th IAK regiments claimed 21 Sabres destroyed (three were listed as lost to MiGs by the USAF).

On 18 and 20 November Maj Nikolay Zameskin was able to increase his victory tally to five, while 224th IAP pilot Capt Boris Siskov (who would become the 52nd, and last, MiG ace) also claimed his first kill on the 18th.

As the winter weather worsened, and MiG units stepped up their patrols, UN fighter-bomber activity in the Pyongyang area reduced still further. But continued attempts to operate to the north of Anju

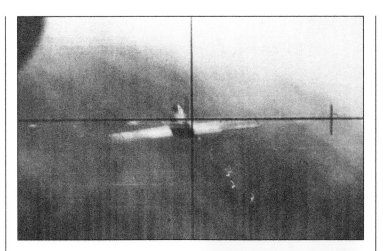

Capt Smirnov (two Korean War victories) of 518th IAP, 216th IAD shot down F-86E-6 52-2841 of the 334th FS/4th FW on 6 October 1952. He closed to within 80 m (85 yrd) of the Sabre before opening fire – the four white twisting lines behind the Sabre are 23 mm gun shells

Hero of the Soviet Union Col Pavel Shevelev, CO of the 415th IAP, 133rd IAD, added three Korean War victories to the 17 kills he had previously scored in World War 2

resulted in MiG pilots claiming four F-84s and six F-80s destroyed (no losses to MiGs were recorded by the USAF). One of the pilots to claim a fighter-bomber kill, on 2 November, was Capt Vasiliy Lepikov of 415th IAP. Two days later he reported downing an F-86 for his all-important fifth victory, but his CO refused to confirm his claim despite subsequent evaluation of gun camera film suggesting that he had indeed destroyed a Sabre (no losses were listed by the USAF).

Hero of the Soviet Union Col Pavel Shevelev, commander of 415th IAP, distinguished himself in one of the battles fought between the MiGs and the Thunderjets that month. Having completed 236 combat missions and fought in 55 aerial battles in World War 2, during which he scored 17 personal and two group victories, he added three more kills over Korea – including an F-84 destroyed and another seriously damaged in a dogfight that took place near Pukchin.

November was also a successful month for 64th IAK nightfighter pilots, who destroyed two bombers. The first was a 19th BG B-29 that crashed in flames into the sea on the 19th after being attacked by Yuriy Dobrovichan of 147th GvIAP. The following night Maj Sichev of Corps Headquarters intercepted a B-26. He spotted the bomber illuminated by searchlights 15 km (nine miles) south of Sinuiju. Sichev twice attacked the Invader and shot it down (no loss was recorded by the USAF), but his opponent's return fire was also accurate. The MiG, with its pilot still strapped into the cockpit, crashed near Pyongyang and exploded. That was the month's second nocturnal loss, for on the night of 6-7 November the MiG-15bis flown by Lt Kovalev of 351st IAP had been intercepted and shot down by an F3D-2 Skynight from US Marine Corps unit VMF(N)-513.

Snr Lt Ikhsangaliev of 351st IAP settles into the cockpit of MiG-15bis 2915376 prior to flying a night sortie. He scored a solitary B-29 kill on 30/31 December 1952

Maj Kultyshev (on ladder), leader of 1st Squadron, 351st IAP, also scored a solitary Korean War victory

December brought more successes for 64th IAK, although once again the MiG pilots rarely encountered US fighter-bombers – just one attack entered the corps' area of responsibility north of Anju. The F-84s succeeded in bombing their targets and escaping unscathed thanks to poor weather keeping the MiGs grounded at their bases. The corps claimed 22 F-86s shot down, however, and lost six MiGs-15bis but no pilots (two Sabres were lost to MiGs according to the USAF, and 29 Soviet jets shot down in return). Amongst the month's successful pilots was future ranking ace of 32nd IAD, Capt Semyon Fedorets, who claimed the first of his seven Korean War victories on 17 December (no F-86s were lost on this date according to USAF records).

64th IAK nightfighters again proved effective as well, with Capt Dobrovichan intercepting a single B-26B of the 3rd BG 20 km (12.5 miles) southeast of Chons on 9 December. He opened fire from 1000 m (1100 yrd) and, closing with the bomber, managed to fire six bursts at it in total. Watching his shells hit the bomber's fuselage and left wing, Dobrovichan got to within 150 m (160 yrd) of the Invader before he ceased firing and the B-26B started descending gradually towards Korea Bay. It eventually crashed into the sea 10 km (six miles) west of Cape Unzenly.

This battle represented the prelude to a series of full-scale nocturnal air engagements which began on 30/31 December and lasted for a fortnight. That night, Superfortresses from the 19th BG tried to attack an ore processing plant in the Tagvan area. Maj Anatoliy Karelin was the first to intercept the B-29s, and he managed to track one of the bombers and place his fighter 400 m (430 yrd) behind it. After several bursts, the B-29's left inner engine caught fire and the blaze quickly engulfed the aircraft and it blew up. Karelin made a rapid climbing right-hand turn, but fragments from the B-29 damaged the left side of his aircraft. Later, shards of duralumin were found lodged in the MiG's gun-bay. Maj Karelin had expended just 40 shells from his H-37 37 mm cannon during the course of this engagement.

Apart from Anatoliy Karelin, Snr Lts Ikhsangaliev, Andreev and Muravyov of 535th IAP each claimed a B-29 destroyed that night. All told, 64th IAK fighter pilots were credited with shooting down four Superfortresses, with two others thought to have been damaged (the USAF reported the loss of just one B-29A).

64th IAK pilots had flown a total of 23,539 daytime and 1062 nocturnal combat sorties during 1952, with 868 daytime group engagements and 32 individual night engagements having taken place. MiG-15 pilots had been credited with 338 victories in total, including 256 Sabres, 37 Thunderjets, 19 Shooting Stars, six Mustangs, three Corsairs, one Meteor F 8, four Invaders and 12 Superfortresses. The corps had lost 160 aircraft and 43 pilots in return.

The battered tail of 39th FS/51st FW F-86F 51-2906, which was shot down by Capt Fedotov of 518th IAP, 216th IAD on 5 December 1952

351st IAP pilot and Hero of the Soviet Union Maj Anatoliy Karelin was credited with downing six B-29s during the Korean War, thus making him the top-scoring Soviet nightfighter pilot of the conflict

JANUARY – JULY 1953

With FEAF Bomber Command's B-29 night offensive continuing into January 1953, it fell to 351st and 535th IAPs to claim the first MiG kills of the new year. On the night of 10/11 January, Maj Kultyshev and Capt Golishevskiy of 351st IAP and Snr Lt Habiev of the 535th IAP were each credited with downing a B-29 – the USAF lost a single 307th BG machine.

On the night of 12/13 January Snr Lt Gubenko of 351st IAP intercepted a Superfortress of the 581st Air Resupply and Communication Wing over Manchuria and shot it down. Less than two hours later, Snr Lt Habiev accounted for an RB-29 from the 91st SRS that was on a leaflet-dropping mission (both losses confirmed by the USAF).

With 64th IAK's modest nightfighter force seeing plenty of action during this period, Maj Anatoliy Karelin, deputy CO of 351st IAP, found no shortage of targets as he became the sole nocturnal MiG ace of the war. Time and again he proved that he was the only Soviet pilot capable of intercepting B-29s without the aid of searchlights. Indeed, the victory Karelin claimed on 28-29 January to 'make ace' was achieved in this way.

Patrolling, near the North Korean capital, he spotted the gleam of the B-29's fuselage in the moonlight. He attacked three times and the 19th BG bomber crashed 50 km (31 miles) southeast of Pyongyang.

On the night of 30/31 January Karelin flew a 'free hunt' in the Pyongyang area. Noticing bombs exploding below him, he looked up and spotted a Superfortress illuminated by moonlight. Having completed its bombing run, the B-29 was making a left turn when Karelin attacked it. He encountered return fire from the bomber's gunners and two bullets hit the MiG's cockpit, damaging the instrument panel. Undaunted, Karelin attacked again. The defensive fire ceased, and he reported seeing the B-29 break up. Karelin made a fourth attack, but due to the damage suffered by his aircraft he was forced to head for home. Nearing Antung, his engine stopped, but Karelin managed to land the damaged fighter.

Later, he received a message saying that the B-29 had crashed 70 km (44 miles) south of Pyongyang – this was the last Superfortress to be destroyed by 64th IAK nightfighter pilots. As the leading Soviet nightfighter ace, Karelin was made a Hero of the Soviet Union on 14 July 1953 by decree of the Presidium of the Supreme Council of the USSR.

On 31 January Snr Lt Kobzev of 535th IAP was credited with the destruction of a B-26 (no losses were recorded by the USAF), this aircraft being 535th IAP's final nocturnal victory of the Korean War. Eight US aircraft had been downed by nightfighter pilots in January, while day fighter regiments were credited with the destruction of 14 F-86s and three F-84s (USAF losses to MiGs were listed as two Sabres and one Thunderjet). Among the successful pilots was Capt Boris Siskov, who was

Nikolay Zameskin (seen here following his promotion to major in the final weeks of the Korean War), who was a squadron leader in 216th IAD's 878th IAP, was also the regiment's sole ace – he claimed six Korean War victories

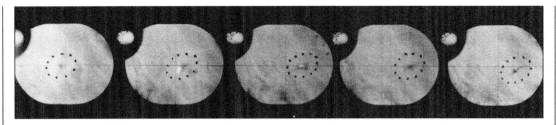

This sequence of camera gun frames was exposed on 4 February 1953 by Capt Zameskin of 878th IAP, 216th IAD. His target is F-86E-10 51-2749 of the 16th FS/51st FW. The second and third frames from the left show the Sabre exploding in mid-air. Zameskin's MiG was damaged by debris from the USAF jet

Capt Nikolay Zameskin pictured in the cockpit of his MiG-15bis 2015363 (side number 263) at Tatung-kao airfield on the morning of 4 February 1953. Five victory stars can just be seen on the fuselage of the jet to the extreme right of this photograph, a sixth star for his victory on this date being applied shortly after this shot was taken

able to add another Sabre kill to his tally. 64th IAK lost five aircraft and two pilots, with an additional 23 MiGs damaged (Sabre pilots claimed 38 MiGs destroyed, with F3D-2 crews getting two more).

In mid-January 32nd and 133rd IADs had swapped bases, with the former moving to Antung and Dapu and the latter re-deploying to Mukden and Anshan. Pilots from both divisions flew high altitude missions, while 216th IAD focused on opposing UN fighter-bombers.

As previously mentioned, UN fighter-bomber units had been struggling to attack targets north of Pyongyang since the autumn of 1952 due to dwindling stocks of F-80s and F-84s and the employment of better tactics by MiG-15 units. 216th IAD's monthly victory tally had declined sharply as a result, but with Sabres now flying more and more fighter-bomber sorties, Soviet pilots began claiming kills again. Indeed, of the 12 F-86s credited to pilots in February (three were listed as lost to MiGs by the USAF), four were attributed to 518th and 878th IAPs.

It was during one such encounter on 4 February that the latter unit's sole ace, Nikolay Zameskin, scored his sixth kill. Six MiGs of the 878th IAP's 3rd Squadron had encountered four Sabres flying parallel with the Yalu River's eastern bank. Squadron CO, HSU Maj Vasiliy Egorov (a World War 2 veteran who had flown 315 combat missions and survived 16 aerial battles with ten individual victories and one group kill to his name – he would claim three more successes in Korea), was leading the unit. Egorov ordered Zameskin and his wingman to cover the rest of the squadron as they attacked. The CO and his wingman, 1Lt Barannikov (two Korean War kills), went for the leading jet of the right-hand pair of Sabres, but they could only fire a short burst prior to them turning sharply and diving away.

Meanwhile, the left-hand pair had been attacked by Capt Kaloshin (one victory in Korea), but again the F-86s shook off their pursuers and latched onto the tail of the Egorov-led element instead. In doing so, they passed directly in front of Zameskin's guns. He opened fire from 200 m (220 yrd), hitting the left wing of the leading F-86. The fighter caught fire and exploded, but debris hit Zameskin's MiG, denting its nose and punching two holes in the canopy (the 51st FW lost an F-86E to MiGs on this date).

32nd IAD claimed the most Sabre kills in February, with Capt Semyon Fedorets adding two more to his tally on the 19th (4th FW lost an F-86E on this date) and 21st (no losses recorded by the USAF). He recalled;

'On 19 February our group was led by Maj Rudakov. After take-off, we climbed up to 13,000 m (42,000 ft) in order to intercept a group of Sabres that had been detected. We were listening attentively to information from our control post on the ground while scanning the sky, hoping to be first to detect the enemy, and thus have the advantage for our initial attack. Success in a fight can depend on such factors.

'Having spotted a group of Sabres to our right and below us, heading in the opposite direction, we turned through 90 degrees and attacked. The regiment stretched out into a single column of flights, and individual element leaders then began deciding on their best point of attack.

'After banking several times, the whole armada descended to 7000-8000 m (22,750-26,000 ft), where the air was denser and the G-loads higher. Then a Sabre latched onto the tail of Valentine Shorin, a pilot in our flight. He put his fighter into an 80-degree climb, and Evgeniy Aseev got in behind the Sabre and fired off several bursts. I flew to the right, 70-100 m (230-325 ft) above Aseev, in support of him. Suddenly, Aseev called "I'm short of ammo" and dropped to the right, under my aircraft.

'I dived and got onto the Sabre's tail. I fired a burst at him from 500 m (540 yrd). The pilot obviously realised that he was in a tight situation and dived. I followed, and from an inverted position closed to within 80 m (85 yrd). I fired a short burst and saw a big orange ball as a cannon shell penetrated the jet's fuselage just behind the cockpit and exploded. Then the fighter dived towards the ground. I put my aircraft into a half-roll to return to level flight and set course for home – the fight was over.'

During February 64th IAK had lost seven aircraft and one pilot, with 24 MiGs damaged (Sabre pilots claimed 22 MiGs destroyed). All losses

Pilots of 913th IAP, 32nd IAD pose for the camera in early 1953. They are, front row, from left to right, Kostenko (three kills), Semyonov (one kill), Razorennov, Marchenko (regimental CO), Popov (two kills), Khoytsev (one kill), Aleksandrov (two kills); second row, from left to right, Karpov (one kill), Efremov (one kill), Shorin, Sotin, Skrykov, Shlyapin (two killa); and third row, from left to right, Nikishov, Maleevskiy (one kill), Aseev (one kill), Pushchin (one kill), Grishenchuk, Zelenskiy, Byvshev (one kill), Ovsaragov and Kiselyov

were incurred by 32nd IAD, whose pilots were inexperienced in formation-strength encounters with F-86s.

Combat continued into March, despite bad weather stopping missions from being flown for extended periods during the month. Again, US fighter-bombers attacked targets south of Pyongyang, although there were occasions when F-84 groups attempted to enlarge their operating area to the north and northwest, thus entering 64th IAK's area of operations. To counter this, MiG pilots conducted 140 'free hunting' sorties. Mornings and evenings, MiGs-15bis in pairs and, occasionally, in bigger elements headed for the east coast of Korea to patrol the Wonsan-Hamhung area, as well as the airspace between Anju and Pyongyang.

Despite flying these patrols, Soviet pilots rarely encountered enemy attack aircraft, and only one clash with F-80s was recorded in March. The Sabres remained the Soviet pilots' main quarry, and Semyon Fedorets of the 913th IAP claimed his fourth victory on 9 March;

'We met three flights of F-86s and the fight started. Aleksandrov, who was leading the second pair, repulsed an attack from the main group and moved left to the second group of Sabres. His wingman, Valentine Shorin, was attacked by two F-86s. He told us about his position, altitude and course. I latched onto one of the jets that was on Shorin's tail and fired a burst. I then followed the other and initially fired my guns at 400 m (430 yrd). I gave the Sabre a follow-up burst from just 100 m. My shells hit the F-86, which caught fire and fell away towards the sea.'

March also saw future ace Capt Grigoriy Berelidze of 224th IAP, 32nd IAD claim his first kills when he downed three F-86s. Pilots from 781st IAP scored their first victories that month too, this regiment having only arrived in Manchuria in February. Part of the 5th Naval Air Force of the Pacific Fleet, based at Primorie and Sakhalin, the regiment had been sent to China without aircraft or technical personnel. Assigned to 216th IAD, the regiment's pilots were thrown into action in late February using the aircraft that had been passed onto them by other units in the division.

The corps' scoreboard for March showed that its pilots had downed ten Sabres and two F-94 Starfires (USAF records state that only two Sabres, and no Starfires, were lost to MiGs). 147th and 298th IAP nightfighters also fought in five engagements with their US counterparts, and although two F-94s were claimed, it is possible that their victims were F3D Skynights (none were lost according to US records). In any case, the victors were 298th IAP's Capt Goncharov during the night of 2/3 March and 147th GvIAP's Capt Zalogin on the night of 3/4 March. 64th IAK lost ten aircraft and four pilots, with 20 MiGs damaged (36 MiGs were claimed by F-86 pilots).

Better weather in April saw UN attack aircraft return to 64th IAK's zone of operations, although only in small groups. The fighter-bomber pilots did their best to take advantage of factors like terrain and bad

Pilots of 878th IAP, 216th IAD relax between missions in early 1953. They are, from left to right, Averin, Prilepov, Nikolaev (three kills) and Voshkin (one kill)

weather during their incursions north of the Chongchon River. They also employed new tactics. F-84s started penetrating MiG Alley at high altitude, covered by fighter sweeps. Once over the target they would dive steeply to attack. These new tactics forced the MiG pilots to fly frequent patrols over potential target areas, and step up the number of free hunts flown over the east coast, as well as south of Anju.

It was during such free hunts that the MiG pilots claimed three F-84s and nine F-86s shot down (USAF losses to MiGs in April totalled one F-84 and six F-86s). Among the victims were such notable aces as Capts Joseph McConnell and Harold Fischer, both from the 39th FS/51st FW. Fischer had scored ten kills by the time he was downed by Capt G N Berelidze and taken prisoner on 7 April (Fischer maintained that his F-86F was brought down by debris from one of two MiGs he claimed to have shot down moments before he was forced to eject). Fischer was Berelidze's fourth victim, the latter recalling here how he downed the ace;

'I was flying in a pair with Leva Kolesnikov. We returned from our mission early, and as we got closer to home, I asked the squadron leader, Mironov, for permission to stay aloft a little longer. He allowed us to remain airborne while the others were landing. When the last aircraft in our group had lowered his undercarriage and started his approach, I noticed we had a "guest". It was a Sabre, which had zoomed up from low altitude to attack the MiG that was landing.

'By that time we were over Dapu, and I heard the following command from our control post – "Who is over the airfield? A Sabre is attacking one of our MiGs – help him!" I looked down and saw two shadows, and naturally assumed that the enemy aircraft was the trailing one. I dived steeply, and when I pulled out and my eyes had cleared, I saw that I was three kilometres behind the enemy and closing in fast. The F-86 pilot noticed me as soon as I came within firing range. He abandoned his target and banked sharply away. But he was too late. I was determined to shoot him down, and I had the experience to do it. The damaged MiG got down successfully on just one undercarriage leg. As for me, after landing I learned that I'd shot down double ace Harold Fischer.'

Capt McConnell had just taken his score to eight when his F-86F was hit by a second MiG and the ace was forced to eject over the Yellow Sea on 12 April – he was quickly rescued by a H-19 helicopter. Pilots from all three regiments of 32nd IAD had participated in this action, and scored five victories – four F-86s and one F-84 (the USAF acknowledged the loss of three Sabres and a Thunderjet to the MiGs, with seven Soviet jets claimed in return). One of the victorious pilots was Maj Semyon Fedorets, who claimed his fifth kill to become 64th IAK's 50th ace;

'The whole division took off to defeat a mass enemy attack on the hydroelectric power station. But my mission was to carry out a free hunt, to keep away from big groups and to pick off enemy aircraft operating individually and in pairs. We took off 15 minutes after the main force. We climbed to 14,000 m (45,500 ft) once in the combat area. From above, against a background of white cloud, we could distinctly see orange flashes from cannon fire, tracer from machine guns and smoke from aircraft that had been shot down. The battle lasted five to seven minutes. Then I heard over the radio, "Help me, I'm being shot down!" Looking around, I noticed a damaged MiG-15 to the right and below me

Capt Grigoriy Berelidze of 224th IAP, 32nd IAD. He shot down five enemy aircraft during the Korean War, including the F-86 of ten-kill ace Capt Harold Fischer on 7 April 1953

at a height of 12,000 m (39,000 ft). The MiG was descending gradually with a pair of F-86s shooting at it.

'I dived and banked sharply to the right, positioning myself immediately behind one of the attacking Sabres. I fired two bursts from above. The first I fired from 200 m, and to make sure I fired another from 100 m. Smoking, the Sabre began to descend.

'During my manoeuvre my wingman, Vasiliy Aleksandrov, and I became separated, and while I was making my attack I heard just one report from him – "The Sabres are behind us". But after that he returned to the airfield and I was alone. Moments later my jet was hit by a burst of fire from above and to the right of me. My instrument panel and canopy were shattered. I moved sharply under the smoking Sabre, which was then 40-50 m ahead and to the left of me. The pilot looked round and saw me – I could see his face so clearly that I could describe it now. He deployed his air brakes, expecting me to overshoot him, but I moved sharply to the Sabre's left and fired. I saw a 37 mm cannon shell hit his right wing centre section. The Sabre lurched to the right, under my aircraft. I don't know how I avoided a collision.

'As soon as I levelled off, I was aware that I was being fired at from behind again – I manoeuvred just in time to dodge the bullets. The first burst had damaged my engine, however, as a cloud of smoke and kerosene poured out the exhaust. Looking round, I saw a pair of Sabres moving in for the kill, and at that moment I realised my aircraft was out of control. It was clear from the way the control column was behaving that the control rods were broken. I had to get out, but opening the canopy proved to be very difficult, and all this time I was being attacked.

'I managed to eject when I was at a height of 11,000 m (35,750 ft), but only opened my 'chute when I had dropped to 2500-2000 m (8000-6500 ft). I could see my stricken, smoking aircraft, and I could see – and hear – four Sabres still firing at it. As I floated down to earth, I remembered that camera gun film was the only way to prove that a kill had indeed been scored! I had been wounded in the left leg prior to ejecting, and I was subsequently hospitalised for nearly two months.'

Fedorets' jet was one of four lost by 64th IAK in April, with 16 more damaged – two pilots were killed. F-86 pilots claimed 26 MiG victories.

In early May US fighter-bomber units again challenged 64th IAK as they increased their sortie tempo in MiG Alley. Soviet fighter pilots managed to counter these incursions during the first half of the month, but by the middle of May MiG regiments were really up against it. F-86F fighter-bombers of the 8th and 18th FBGs had begun appearing in-theatre in late February, and unlike the F-51s, F-80s and F-84s that had previously flown the bulk of these attack missions, the Sabres became formidable fighters once they had dropped their bombs.

With more than 250 F-86s now in South Korea, Soviet losses began to rise. During May, 64th IAK lost 11 MiGs-15bis and three pilots, although in several cases pilots were forced to eject because their aircraft had run out of fuel (no fewer than 58 MiGs were claimed to have been destroyed by Sabre pilots). MiG pilots claimed nine Sabres and one Thunderjet shot down in return, while a second F-84 and an F-94 fell to the guns of 298th IAP's nightfighter pilots (both F-84s, the F-94 and two Sabres fell to MiGs according to USAF records).

Capt Semyon Fedorets of 913th IAP, 32nd IAD was credited with seven Korean War victories, making him the division's top ace

One of the Sabres credited to 64th IAK was a 4th FW jet downed by Maj Zhuravel of 518th IAP (four Korean War victories) on 17 May. His flight was covering other MiGs landing at Tatung-kao when Zhuravel spotted a Sabre about a kilometre away, heading north at high speed from Korea Bay at an altitude of 1500 m (5000 ft). Zhuravel hauled his jet around in a sharp left turn, only to discover another F-86 on his tail. A rapid right turn then put him 80 m behind the trailing Sabre, and he opened fire at close range and shot the aircraft down.

June was to be the most fruitful month for 64th IAK in terms of aerial victories, as its pilots were credited with downing 36 F-86s, four F-84s and one F-80 – remarkably, the USAF stated that only a single Sabre was lost to MiGs! In addition, 298th IAP nightfighter pilots destroyed a Thunderjet. But the cost of these successes had been high, with 24 MiGs-15bis lost and ten pilots killed and 15 MiGs damaged (Sabre pilots claimed an amazing 77 MiGs destroyed). Of this total, five aircraft and three pilots had fallen to F-86s while taking off or landing.

On 5 June Capt Grigoriy Berelidze scored his fifth victory in Korea;

'Six F-86s suddenly attacked our group from above, but they were being tracked by Leva Kolesnikov. Facing the enemy attack, Leva separated from me, and I found myself alone against the last pair of Sabres. Spotting a fighter on my tail, I made a sudden manoeuvre to spoil his aim. The lower weight and higher thrust of my MiG-15bis in comparison with the Sabre allowed me to get above him and close in. I attacked the lead F-86 and destroyed it.'

Berelidze's group had been attacked by Sabres escorting the now ever-present fighter-bombers that did their utmost to exploit the poor weather conditions that blighted operations throughout June. USAF jets attempted to replicate the success they had enjoyed when attacking the Suphun hydroelectric power station in June of the previous year. The Antung bridge also remained a priority target, and UN aircraft attacked airfields under construction in North Korea too. In response, corps fighter pilots were particularly active in patrolling these areas during June.

32nd IAD was assigned the task of defending the power station, while 216th IAD provided an air umbrella over the Antung bridge. Bad weather, which prevented the fighters from fully exploiting their speed capability,

Maj Zhuravel of 518th IAP fires at 4th FW F-86F 51-12962 with all his cannon from a range of just 85 m on 17 May 1953. This blow-up of the second frame of Zhuravel's film shows twisting white lines in front of the Sabre, which are the 37 mm and 23 mm shells from his cannon. The F-86 crashed shortly after this image was taken

was one of the negative factors contributing to the month's high loss rate amongst the regiments. Even so, MiG pilots successfully intercepted fighter-bombers approaching their areas of responsibility. Semyon Fedorets recalled one incident;

'On 10 June six of us were to provide air cover for the Suphun power station. Several minutes later we saw eight Sabres ahead of us. We could see them clearly against the blue sky, as they were 1000 m above us. I attacked the leader of the first element. I fired several bursts from less than 200 m and hit his left wing

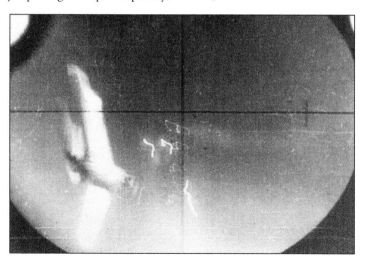

Pilots of 878th IAP, 216th IAD relax at Ulumbey health centre in June 1953. The following aviators scored victories in the Korean War – first row, reclining, flight leader Capt Lomasov (1), deputy squadron leader Capt Skorov (2); second row, first and second from left, Snr Lt Brazhnikov (1) and squadron leader Capt Seliverstov (2); centre of second row, regimental CO Lt Col Dronov (3); third row, flight leader Capt Voshkin (second left, 1 kill victory), flight leader Snr Lt Antontsev (first on the right, 2 kills); fourth row, extreme left, assistant regimental CO Capt Semyonov (1); fourth row, second and third from the left, squadron political officer Snr Lt Barannikov (2) and deputy squadron leader Capt Kaloshin, and extreme right, deputy regimental CO, Hero of the Soviet Union Maj Egorov (three Korean War victories and 11 in World War 2)

centre-section. The Sabre broke up and my aircraft started to shake, so I slackened my speed.

'After I landed I saw that there was a big hole in the left side of the fuselage and an even bigger hole, some 25-30 cm in diameter, in the wing. The Sabre's left wing slat, weighing 3 kg (6 lb), had sliced through the fuselage, holed the wing and lodged near the main-spar. The regimental commander was glad. He told the technicians "Maj Fedorets has saved us from having to search for the wreckage of the aircraft he shot down. He's brought back the evidence himself!" My damaged jet was taken to be repaired and I was given another. That was my penultimate victory.'

The final month of the Korean War was a particularly difficult time for Soviet pilots. Accumulated combat fatigue and disadvantageous operating conditions contributed to the high loss rate. Some 15 MiGs were shot down, with four pilots lost and eight aircraft damaged (Sabre pilots claimed 33 kills). A third of the losses were incurred on landing or take off, while half of the ten victories (USAF recorded just two F-86s lost to MiGs) credited to MiG pilots over Sabres were scored near corps bases.

On 19 July Semyon Fedorets claimed his seventh, and last, Korean War victory over Dapu airfield (no F-86s were lost on this date according to the USAF). The following day, six 224th IAP MiGs flew an uneventful patrol in the Suphun area. At about 1300 hrs the Soviet fighters were back over their home base. The group commander and his wingman were the first to land, followed by the second pair, leaving Capt Boris Siskov and his wingman, Snr Lt Klimov, alone in the air.

The latter two had descended to 150 m, and were just about to land, when the range-finder sensor device installed in Vladimir Klimov's jet started to ring in his headset – this system was actuated when it detected the Sabre's target range-finder. Moments later Siskov warned Klimov to clear his tail. Below the MiGs were a pair of Sabres, their smoky exhausts indicating that they were heading for them at full-throttle.

The MiGs made a steep left-hand climbing turn. The Americans tried to do likewise, but their speed was 300 kmh (190 mph) faster, and they passed into the gunsights of the Soviet fighters. The lead F-86 was attacked by Boris Siskov, and the 4th FG jet crashed near the MiGs' base. The second Sabre escaped Vladimir Klimov's fire by flying into a bank of low cloud. Siskov's victory was his fifth, and final, kill, making him the last of 52 MiG pilots to achieve acedom with 64th IAK in Korea.

Fighter pilots from the 781st IAP were in action three hours later when they fought F-86s over Tatung-kao airfield. Two Sabres were claimed to have been shot down (only one loss was listed by the USAF), and these became the final Soviet fighter kills of the Korean War.

During 1953, 64th IAK pilots had completed 18,152 day and 1373 nocturnal sorties, fought 508 day and 59 nocturnal air battles and been credited with 123 victories – 100 F-86s, 12 F-84s, one F-80, three F-94s and seven B-29s. In turn, 76 MiGs and 26 pilots had been lost.

On 14 July 1953, aces Arkadiy Boytsov, Anatoliy Karelin and Mikhail Mikhin were made Heroes of the Soviet Union for their successful combat operations in Korea in 1952-53 – during this period, 16 64th IAK fighter pilots had become aces. Many others would have probably also done so if their claims had been confirmed under the system used in 1950-51. Following a tightening up in the kill confirmation criteria in mid-1952, the results achieved by pilots in the final year of the conflict were more modest than those of their predecessors.

Between 1 November 1950 and 27 July 1953, Soviet fighter pilots in Manchuria flew 60,450 day and 2779 night combat sorties, and fought in 1683 daytime group air battles and 107 individual night battles. 64th IAK's pilots scored 1097 victories as follows – 65 B-29s, seven B-26s, two RB-45s, one RB-50, two F-47s, 28 F-51s, 118 F-80s, 185 F-84s, 647 F-86s, 11 F-94s, one F4U, three F6Fs, one F3D and 26 Meteor F 8s. Total losses were 335 aircraft and 120 pilots, including 319 aircraft and 110 pilots in aerial combat. These figures are taken from official 64th IAK documentation, having initially been derived from reports created by the corps' divisions and regiments.

On the basis of kills attributable to individual pilots, after all necessary confirmations have been taken into account, the total becomes 1025 – 66 B-29s, seven B-26s, two RB-45s, one RB-50, two F-47s, 28 F-51s, 123 F-80s, 181 F-84s, 574 F-86s, 11 F-94s, one F4U, three F6Fs and 26 Meteor F 8s. Combat losses amounted to 307 aircraft and 103 pilots.

For over half a century, Western sources have portrayed the skies over Korea between 1950 and 1953 as being something of a playground for US fighter pilots, who were able to achieve an impressive kill ratio over opponents who were assumed to be mainly North Koreans or Chinese, with a leavening of Soviet 'volunteers'. The reality, as the authors have attempted to show in this volume, was somewhat different.

Not only were the MiG-15s operated by regular Soviet Air Force units constantly rotating through the combat zone, but many of their pilots were capable of making life difficult for the USAF. Indeed, just like their US counterparts, many had combat experience in World War 2 to draw on. All told, 52 Soviet MiG-15 pilots downed five enemy aircraft, with thirteen downing ten or more. For these achievements they are entitled to be regarded as the MiG-15 aces of the Korean War.

Maj Mikheev (four Korean War victories) and Capt Mikhin (nine victories) of 518th IAP, 216th IAD, seen here at war's end

APPENDICES

64th IAK Units during the Korean War

Division and Regiment	Period in action	Airfield
151st GvIAD	1/11/50 – 30/11/50 and 6/2/51 – 2/4/51	
28th GvIAP		Mukden from 11/50 and Antung from 6/2/51
72nd GvIAP		Anshan from 11/50
28th IAD	1/11/50 – 30/11/50	
67th IAP		Liaoyang
139th GvIAP		Liaoyang
50th IAD	25/11/50 – 6/2/51	
29th GvIAP		Anshan from 25/11/50 and Antung from 3/12/50
177th IAP		Anshan from 25/11/50 and Antung from 15/12/50 (one squadron) and from 25/12/50 (whole regiment)
324th IAD	3/4/51 – 30/1/52	
176th GvIAP		Antung from 2/4/51
196th IAP		Antung from 3/4/51
303rd IAD	8/5/51 – 20/2/52	
17th IAP		Tatung-kao from 11/6/51
18th GvIAP		Antung from 8/5/51 and Tatung-kao from 5/7/51
523rd IAP		Tatung-kao from 28/5/51
97th IAD	25/1/52 – 28/8/52	
16th IAP		Antung from 25/1/52 and Mukden-West from 13/5/52
148th GvIAP		Antung from 25/1/52, Tatung-kao from 30/3/51, Antung from 5/5/52 and Mukden-West from 5/7/52
190th IAD	14/2/52 – 10/8/52	
256th IAP		Tatung-kao from 14/2/52, Anshan from 25/5/52 and Dapu from 30/6/52
494th IAP		Tatung-kao from 14/2/52, Antung from 30/3/52, Anshan from 5/5/52 and Tatung-kao from 25/5/52
821st IAP		Tatung-kao from 14/02/52
133rd IAD	15/5/52 – 27/7/53	
147th GvIAP		Tatung-kao from 15/5/52, Mukden-West from 29/4/53 (nightfighter squadron), Antung from 5/7/52 and Mukden-West from 13/1/53 (day fighter squadrons)
415th IAP		Antung from 9/7/52, Dapu from 16/8/52 and Mukden-West from 20/1/53
726th IAP		Dapu from 12/7/52, Antung from 16/8/52 and Anshan from 20/1/53
578th IAP (Pacific Fleet Air Force)	26/9/52 – 16/2/53	Antung from 26/9/52 and Mukden-West from 23/1/53 (arrived without aircraft and groundcrew, and pilots flew aircraft of superseded division)

216th IAD	30/7/52 – 27/7/53	
518th IAP		Tatung-kao
676th IAP		Dapu
878th IAP		Tatung-kao
781st IAP (Pacific Fleet Air Force)	21/2/53 – 27/7/53	Tatung-kao and Dapu (arrived without aircraft and groundcrew, and pilots flew aircraft of superseded division)
32nd IAD	27/8/52 – 27/7/53	
224th IAP		Mukden-West from 27/8/52, Dapu from 20/1/53 and Antung from 10/4/53
535th IAP		Mukden-West from 27/8/52, Antung from 20/1/53 and Dapu from 10/4/53
913th IAP		Anshan from 27/8/52 and Antung from 24/1/53
351st IAP (nightfighter)	9/9/51 – 16/2/53	Anshan and Antung
298th IAP (nightfighter)	20/2/53 – 27/7/53	Tatung-kao, Antung from 5/53 (two squadrons) and Tatung-kao (one squadron)

Soviet Korean War Aces

(Ranked in date order of fifth victory)

No.	Rank	Name	Regiment	Division	Date of fifth victory	Total number of victories	Number and type of enemy aircraft shot down
1	Capt	S I Naumenko	29th GvIAP	50th IAD	24/12/50	5	1 B-29, 2 F-84s, 2 F-86s
2	Lt Col	V I Kolyadin	28th GvIAP	151st GvIAD	19/3/51	5	2 B-29s, 1 F-51, 2 F-86s
3	Snr Lt	F A Shebanov	196th IAP	324th IAD	22/4/51	6	1 B-29, 5 F-86s
4	Maj	S P Subbotin	176th GvIAP	324th IAD	18/6/51	9	2 B-29s, 1 Meteor F 8, 1 F-80, 2 F-84s, 3 F-86s
5	Capt	G I Ges	176th GvIAP	324th IAD	20/6/51	8	1 B-26, 1 B-29, 1 Meteor F 8, 1 F-51, 2 F-80s, 1 F-84, 1 F-86
6	Capt	S M Kramarenko	176th GvIAP	324th IAD	11/7/51	13	2 Meteor F 8s, 2 F-80s, 9 F-86s
7	Maj	N V Sutyagin	17th IAP	303rd IAD	29/7/51	22	2 Meteor F 8s, 2 F-80s, 3 F-84s, 15 F-86s
8	Snr Lt	G T Shatalov	523rd IAP	303rd IAD	10/9/51	5	2 F-51s, 1 F-80, 2 F-86s
9	Maj	M S Ponomarev	17th IAP	303rd IAD	11/9/51	12	3 F-80s, 6 F-84s, 3 F-86s
10	Capt	G U Okhay	523rd IAP	303rd IAD	11/9/51	11	3 Meteor F 8s, 2 F-80s, 2 F-84s, 4 F-86s
11	Capt	N K Shelamonov	196th IAP	303rd IAD	12/9/51	5	1 RB-45, 2 F-80s, 1 F-86, 1 F-94
12	Lt Col	A N Karasev	523rd IAP	303rd IAD	19/9/51	7	1 B-29, 1 F-80, 4 F-84s, 1 F-86
13	Capt	L K Shchukin	18th GvIAP	303rd IAD	20/9/51	15	2 Meteor F 8s, 1 F-51, 2 F-80s, 5 F-84s, 5 F-86s
14	Maj	S A Bakhaev	523rd IAP	303rd IAD	26/09/51	11	1 B-29, 3 F-80s, 2 F-84s, 5 F-86s
15	Lt Col	G I Pulov	17th IAP	303rd IAD	6/10/51	8	1 Meteor F 8, 2 F-80s, 1 F-84, 4 F-86s
16	Col	E G Pepelyaev	196th IAP	324th IAD	6/10/51	19	1 F-80, 2 F-84s, 14 F-86s, 2 F-94s
17	Maj	K Ya Sheberstov	176th GvIAP	324th IAD	6/10/51	12	1 B-29, 1 F-51, 2 F-80s, 2 F-84s, 6 F-86s

No.	Rank	Name	Regiment	Division	Date of fifth victory	Total number of victories	Number and type of enemy aircraft shot down
18	Lt Col	A P Smorchkov	18th GvIAP	303rd IAD	10/10/51	12	3 B-29s, 3 F-80s, 2 F-84s, 4 F-86s
19	Snr Lt	D A Samoylov	523rd IAP	303rd IAD	12/10/51	10	1 B-29, 2 F-84s, 7 F-86s
20	Maj	D P Oskin	523rd IAP	303rd IAD	23/10/51	15	2 B-29s, 2 Meteor F 8s, 1 F-80, 4 F-84s, 6 F-86s
21	Capt	L N Ivanov	196th IAP	324th IAD	26/10/51	7	2 F-80s, 5 F-86s
22	Maj	P N Antonov	18th GvIAP	303rd IAD	27/10/51	7	1 F-80, 2 F-84s, 4 F-86s
23	Capt	N G Dokashenko	17th IAP	303rd IAD	28/10/51	9	1 F6F-5, 8 F-86s
24	Capt	N L Kornienko	18th GvIAP	303rd IAD	30/10/51	5	1 B-29, 1 F-80, 2 F-84s, 1 F-86
25	Capt	I A Suchkov	176th GvIAP	324th IAD	4/11/51	10	2 B-29s, 2 F-80s, 2 F-84s, 4 F-86s
26	Capt	V F Shulev	17th IAP	303rd IAD	4/11/51	7	1 F-84, 6 F-86s
27	Maj	S S Artemchenko	17th IAP	303rd IAD	23/11/51	6	1 F-80, 1 F-84, 4 F-86s
28	Capt	P S Milaushkin	176th GvIAP	324th IAD	24/11/51	11	1 B-29, 2 Meteor F 8s, 3 F-84s, 5 F-86s
29	Col	S F Vishnyakov	176th GvIAP	324th IAD	5/12/51	6	1 Meteor F 8, 1 F-51, 2 F-84s, 2 F-86s
30	Capt	B S Abakumov	196th IAP	324th IAD	5/12/51	5	1 F-80, 3 F-86s, 1 F-94
31	Capt	V N Alfeev	196th IAP	324th IAD	11/12/51	7	1 F-80, 1 F-84, 5 F-86s
32	Capt	B V Bokach	196th IAP	324th IAD	11/12/51	6	1 F-84, 5 F-86s
33	Snr Lt	V I Stepanov	18th GvIAP	303rd IAD	13/12/51	5	1 B-29, 2 F-84s, 2 F-86s
34	Maj	A A Kalyuzhniy	Headquarters	303rd IAD	13/12/51	6	1 F6F-5, 1 F-84, 4 F-86s
35	Lt Col	A I Mitusov	196th IAP	324th IAD	27/12/51	7	1 F-80, 1 F-84, 5 F-86s
36	Capt	N M Goncharov	196th IAP	324th IAD	28/12/51	5	1 F-84, 3 F-86s, 1 F-94
37	Capt	Bychkov	17th IAP	303rd IAD	6/1/52	5	1 B-29, 2 F-84s, 2 F-86s
38	Capt	I M Zaplavnev	196th IAP	324th IAD	7/1/52	7	1 F-80, 1 F-84, 5 F-86s
39	Capt	V G Muravyov	196th IAP	324th IAD	11/1/52	5	1 F-80, 4 F-86s
40	Capt	N S Volkov	17th IAP	303rd IAD	11/1/52	7	1 F-80, 1 F-84, 5 F-86s
41	Capt	V P Popov	523rd IAP	303rd IAD	19/1/52	5	1 F-80, 2 F-84s, 2 F-86s
42	Maj	V M Zabelin	821st IAP	190th IAD	13/4/52	9	1 F-84, 8 F-86s
43	Maj	A A Olenitsa	821st IAP	190th IAD	17/5/52	5	1 F-51, 1 F-80, 2 F-84s, 1 F-86
44	Maj	A T Bashman	148th GvIAP	97th IAD	31/5/52	5	1 F-51, 4 F-86s
45	Maj	A S Boytsov	16th IAP	97th IAD	11/7/52	6	2 F-84s, 4 F-86s
46	Maj	G F Dmitryuk	821st IAP	190th IAD	11/7/52	5	1 F-80, 1 F-84, 3 F-86s
47	Capt	M I Mikhin	518th IAP	216th IAD	9/9/52	9	1 F-84, 8 F-86s
48	Maj	N M Zameskin	878th IAP	216th IAD	20/11/52	6	6 F-86s
49	Maj	A M Karelin	351st IAP	Independent	28/1/53	6	6 B-29s
50	Maj	S A Fedorets	913th IAP	32nd IAD	12/4/53	7	7 F-86s
51	Capt	G N Berelidze	224th IAP	32nd IAD	5/6/53	5	5 F-86s
52	Capt	B N Siskov	224th IAP	32nd IAD	20/7/53	5	5 F-86s

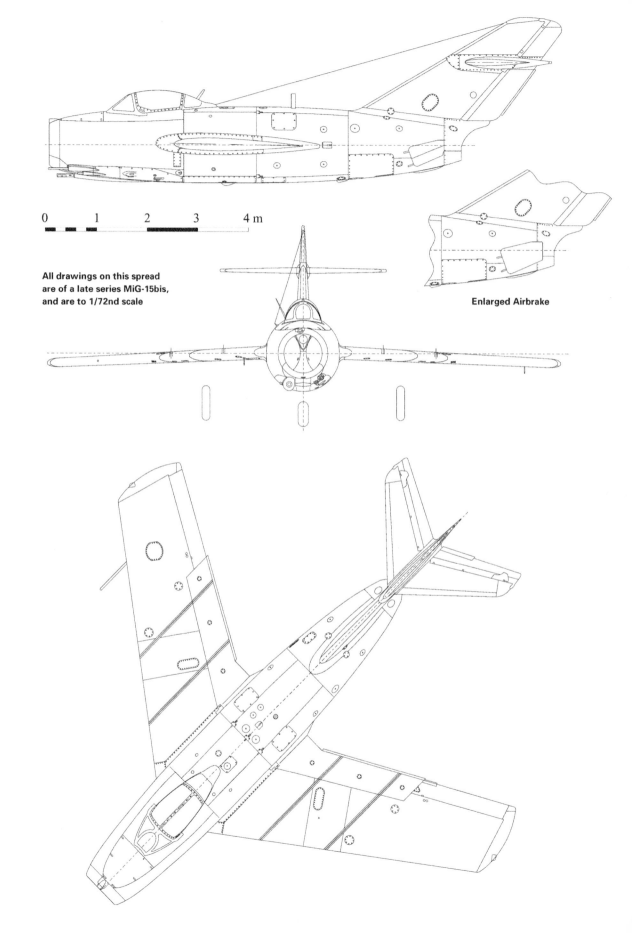

0   1   2   3   4 m

All drawings on this spread
are of a late series MiG-15bis,
and are to 1/72nd scale

Enlarged Airbrake

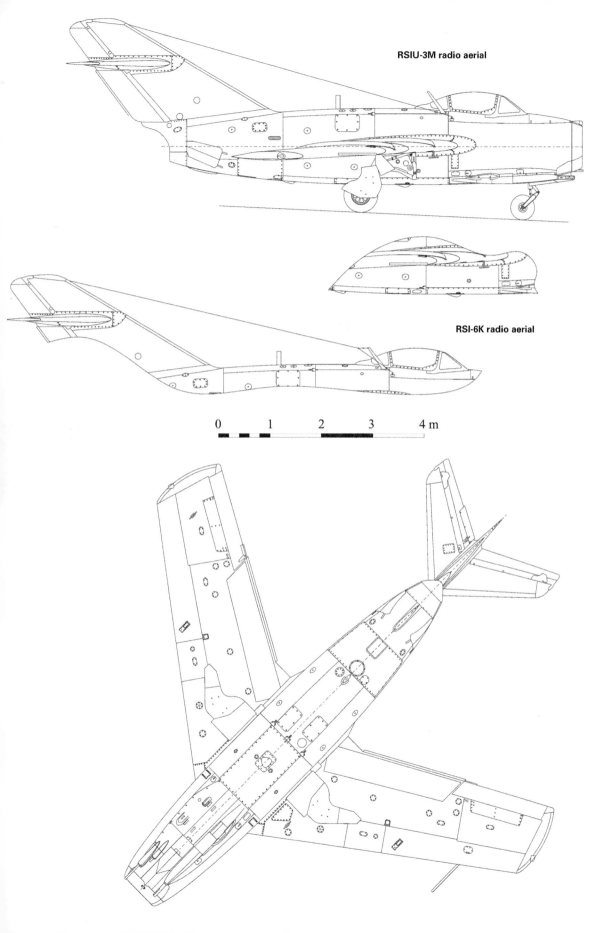

RSIU-3M radio aerial

RSI-6K radio aerial

0   1   2   3   4 m

1

MiG-15 0615354 of Maj N V Stroykov, 72nd GvIAP, Anshan, 1 November 1950

This aircraft was built by Factory No 153 at Novosibirsk and flown by the 1st Squadron CO, HSU Maj Stroykov. On 1 November 1950 he led a group of 72nd GvIAP pilots during their first combat sortie, and the MiG-15's first aerial engagement of the Korean War. This aircraft was handed over to 9th IAP, 3rd IAD of the Chinese Air Force in late January 1951.

2

MiG-15 11811 of Lt V I Chizh, 72nd GvIAP, Anshan, 1 November 1950

The aircraft was built by Factory No 1 at Kuybyshev. On 1 November 1950, the 1st Squadron's Lt V I Chizh (a 13-victory ace from World War 2) was flying it when he became the first Soviet pilot to be credited with an aerial victory in the Korean War. He claimed an F-51D Mustang shot down during the combat sortie led by Maj Stroykov. In late January 1951 the aircraft was handed over to 9th IAP, 3rd IAD of the Chinese Air Force.

3

MiG-15 0615356 of Maj Bordun, 72nd GvIAP, Anshan, 1 November 1950

Built by Factory No 153 at Novosibirsk, this aircraft was flown by 2nd Squadron CO Maj Bordun on 1 November 1950, when he led a group of 72nd GvIAP aircraft in the first ever jet-versus-jet dogfight. Soviet pilots claimed a kill during the clash with USAF F-80 Shooting Stars. This MiG-15 was also eventually passed on to the Chinese-manned 9th IAP, 3rd IAD in late January 1951.

4

MiG-15 0615372 of Snr Lt Khominich, 72nd GvIAP, Anshan, 1 November 1950

Snr Lt Khominich of the 2nd Squadron was flying this aircraft, built by Factory No 153 at Novosibirsk, when he too claimed an F-80 destroyed on 1 November 1950. Again, this MiG-15 was subsequently handed over to 9th IAP, 3rd IAD in late January 1951.

5

MiG-15 0615334 of Maj V I Kolyadin, 28th GvIAP, Mukden-West, November 1950

Future five-kill MiG ace, and CO of 28th GvIAP, HSU Maj V I Kolyadin flew this aircraft in November 1950. Built by Factory No 153 at Novosibirsk, this MiG-15 was passed on to 8th IAP, 3rd IAD of the Chinese Air Force in late January 1951.

6

MiG-15 120125 of Capt Grachyov, 139th GvIAP, Liaoyang, 9 November 1950

1st Squadron CO Capt Grachyov was flying this aircraft, built by Factory No 1, when he was shot down and killed by Lt Cdr W T Amen of VF-111 during a dogfight with US Navy F9F-2 Panthers on 9 November 1950. Grachyov was the first Soviet

pilot to be killed in action in Korea, and his MiG-15 the first to be lost in combat.

7

MiG-15bis 0715323 of Capt S I Naumenko, 29th GvIAP, Antung, January 1951

Built by Factory No 153 in September 1950, this aircraft was duly passed on to 29th GvIAP and flown by deputy squadron leader Capt Naumenko from October of that same year. He became the first Soviet pilot to score five aerial victories in the Korean War when he claimed his fifth kill on 24 December 1950. In February 1951 the jet was transferred to 72nd GvIAP, and two months later it joined 196th IAP. In January 1952 0715323 went to 16th IAP, where it was attached to a 97th IAD nightfighter squadron. In April of that year the aircraft was transferred to 726th IAP, and on 6 September it was handed over to a Soviet Air Force regiment that did not participate in the Korean War.

8

MiG-15bis 0615396 of Capt Nikolay Vorobyov, 177th IAP, Antung, 22 December 1950

Built by Factory No 153 in August 1950, this aircraft was issued to 177th IAP's deputy squadron leader Capt Vorobyov in October of that same year. And it was while flying this aircraft on 22 December 1950 that Capt Vorobyov shot down F-86A 49-1176 of the 4th FW. In doing so, Vorobyov, who scored two Korean War victories, had become the first Soviet pilot to down a Sabre in the Korean War. In February 1951 0615396 was handed over to 28th GvIAP, 151st GvIAD, and two months later it joined 196th IAP, 324th IAD. On 20 May 1951, Capt Nazarkin (three Korean War victories) was shot down by an F-86 whilst flying this jet.

9

MiG-15 109025 of Lt Col E G Pepelyaev, 196th IAP, Antung, April 1951

Built by Factory No 1 at Kuybyshev, this aircraft entered service with the headquarters of 196th IAP and was flown by the regimental CO, Lt Col Pepelyaev, during his first combat sorties in April 1951. Later that same month 109025 was transferred to 151st GvIAD, and on 6 October it was handed over to 447th IAP, 435th IAD of the North Korean Air Force.

10

MiG-15bis 0715368 of Lt Col E G Pepelyaev, 196th IAP, Antung, May 1951

This aircraft was built by Factory No 153 in September 1950 and initially issued to 29th GvIAP, where it was flown from November onwards by the deputy regimental CO, Maj Bersenev. In late January 1951 0715368 was handed over to 72nd GvIAP, and three months later it was passed on to 196th IAP, 324th IAD. During April and May 1951 the fighter was flown by the CO of 196th IAP, Lt Col Pepelyaev, before being assigned to Snr Lt Khimchenko of 196th IAP in late May. In January 1952 0715368 was transferred to 148th GvIAP and then to 351st IAP, and on 30 September 1952 it joined 147th GvIAP, before returning to 351st IAP on

6 October. Later in the month the MiG was passed on to 518th IAP, where it remained until handed over to 100th IAD shortly before war's end. The aircraft was transferred to the Chinese Air Force in November 1954.

11

MiG-15bis 1315325 of Lt Col E G Pepelyaev, 196th IAP, Antung, June 1951 to January 1952

This aircraft, built by Factory No 153 in April 1951, was assigned the following month to the CO of 196th IAP, Lt Col Pepelyaev, who used it to score at least 17 of his 19 Korean War victories. In late January 1952 it went to 16th IAP and was assigned to Capt Minervin, who claimed three Korean War victories, including one achieved while flying this aircraft. In March 1952 1315325 was transferred to 351st IAP, and Capt A M Karelin was flying it when he downed two B-29s and damaged another on 10 June. In October 1952 the fighter was transferred to 415th IAP and assigned to Snr Lt Sokurenko, who scored both his victories while flying it. Soon after war's end the aircraft went to 37th IAD, and in November 1954 it was passed on to the Chinese Air Force.

12

MiG-15bis 1815399 of Lt Col E G Pepelyaev, 196th IAP, Antung, 1 December 1951

Another Factory No 153-built aircraft, this fighter emerged in October 1951 and was assigned to 196th IAP, where it was flown by deputy regimental CO Maj A I Mitusov (seven Korean War victories). It was while flying this aircraft that regimental CO Lt Col Pepelyaev shot down F-80C 49-0855 of the 8th FBG on 1 December 1951. In late January 1952 the jet was handed over to 16th IAP, and in March to 494th IAP. On 11 August 1815399 was transferred to 518th IAP and assigned to Snr Lt Lapitskiy, and 12 months later, on 12 August 1953, the jet was passed on to 100th IAD after this division relieved 216th IAD in Manchuria.

13

MiG-15 111035 of Capt S M Kramarenko, 176th GvIAP, Antung, 12 April 1951

In April 1951 this Factory No 1-built aircraft was assigned to 13-kill ace Capt Kramarenko. Later that same month it was transferred to 151st GvIAD and then, on 6 October 1951, to 447th IAP, 435th IAD of the North Korean Air Force.

14

MiG-15bis 0715329 of Capt S M Kramarenko, 176th GvIAP, Antung, May 1951 to January 1952

0715329 was built by Factory No 153 in September 1950 and entered service with 29th GvIAP the following month. In January 1951 it went to 72nd GvIAP and in April to 176th GvIAP, where the fighter was assigned to Capt Kramarenko. In January 1952 the aircraft was passed on to 148th GvIAP, in March to 821st IAP and in August to 878th IAP. On 26 September 1952, while being flown by Snr Lt Orlov, 0715329 was shot down during a dogfight with an F-86.

15

MiG-15bis 0615389 of Snr Lt F A Shebanov, 196th IAP, Antung, 20 May 1951

Built by Factory No 153 in August 1950, this aircraft entered the inventory of 177th IAP the following October. In February 1951 it was handed over to 28th GvIAP and in late April it was fielded by 196th IAP and assigned to Snr Lt Shebanov, who used it on 20 May 1951 to score his sixth, and last, victory of the Korean War. Shebanov was killed while flying this aircraft on 26 October 1951 during a dogfight with a USAF F-84.

16

MiG-15bis 121032 of Capt N V Sutyagin, 17th IAP, Tatung-kao, June 1951 to January 1952

Ranking Soviet ace Nikolay Sutyagin of 17th IAP scored all 22 of his Korean War victories while flying this aircraft, which was built by Factory No 1 in June 1950. On 28 January 1952 the fighter was handed over to 190th IAD and entered the inventory of 821st IAP. On 9 August 1952 121032 was transferred to 878th IAP and assigned to Snr Lt Opryshko, who scored three Korean War victories with it.

17

MiG-15bis 121067 of Snr Lt D A Samoylov, 523rd IAP, Tatung-kao, June 1951 to January 1952

Snr Lt Samoylov, who was credited with ten Korean War victories, was assigned this aircraft, which was built by Factory No 1 in July 1950 and then delivered to 523rd IAP. The fighter was handed over to 256th IAP on 21 January 1952 and flown by Capt Sinitsyn (one Korean War victory) and Snr Lt Krasulin (two victories) until the latter was shot down and killed whilst flying it during an engagement with a Sabre on 25 May 1952.

18

MiG-15bis 123045 of Lt Col A P Smorchkov, 18th GvIAP, Tatung-kao, May 1951 to January 1952

This aircraft was built by Factory No 1 in July 1950, delivered to the headquarters of 18th GvIAP on 20 December 1950 and flown by deputy regimental CO Lt Col Smorchkov. And it was while flying this aircraft that Smorchkov, who achieved four combat kills during World War 2 and 12 during the Korean War, engaged Superfortresses on 22 and 23 October 1952. The aircraft was subsequently handed over to 821st IAP on 7 February 1952.

19

MiG-15bis 123051 of Maj D P Oskin, 18th GvIAP, Tatung-kao, September 1951

Maj Oskin, who achieved 15 Korean War victories, was assigned this aircraft on 5 January 1951. It had been built by Factory No 1 the previous August and issued to the headquarters of 18th GvIAP. In October 1951 Maj Oskin was made CO of 523rd IAP, and the fighter passed to Snr Lt Voistinnykh, who achieved one Korean War kill. 123051 was also handed over to 821st IAP on 7 February 1952.

20

MiG-15bis 121026 of Capt N G Dokashenko, 17th IAP, Tatung-kao, late January 1952

This fighter is depicted as it appeared during trials of various camouflage schemes for MiG-15bis in service with 64th IAK. The aircraft was built by Factory No 1 in Kuybyshev in July 1950, delivered to 17th IAP and in January 1951 assigned to flight leader Capt Dokashenko, who achieved nine Korean

War victories. 121026 was handed over to 494th IAP on 28 January 1952 and, while piloted by Snr Lt Chernykh, the MiG was shot down during a dogfight with F-84s and F-86s on 4 July.

21

MiG-15bis 0515381 of Capt V M Khvostantsev, 17th IAP, Tatung-kao, late January 1952

This aircraft, built by Factory No 153 in July 1950, is also shown in one of the trial camouflage schemes tried out by 64th IAK MiG-15bis fighters. 0515381 had been delivered to 17th IAP in December 1950 and assigned to flight leader Capt Khvostantsev, who went on to score four Korean War kills. The fighter was handed over to 494th IAP on 28 January 1952, and on 29 April it was transferred to 726th IAP. On 6 September 1952 0515381 was passed on to a Soviet unit that did not take part in the Korean War.

22

MiG-15bis 0415399 of Capt N S Volkov, 17th IAP, Tatung-kao, late January 1952

Built by Factory No 153 in July 1950, this aircraft was issued to 17th IAP and assigned to seven-kill ace Capt Volkov five months later. The fighter is depicted here in one of the various camouflage schemes tested by 64th IAK. Having been transferred to 494th IAP on 28 January 1952, the jet was shot down during a dogfight with USAF F-86s on 11 March 1952. Its pilot, Snr Lt Zinakov, ejected successfully.

23

MiG-15bis 121083 of Snr Lt Nikolaev, 17th IAP, Tatung-kao, late January 1952

Built by Factory No 1 in June 1950, this aircraft was fielded by 17th IAP and assigned in January 1951 to Snr Lt Nikolaev. A pilot in Capt N G Dokashenko's flight, Nikolaev went on to achieve four Korean War kills. The fighter is shown here in one of the camouflage schemes tested by 64th IAK, following which, on 28 January 1952, it was handed over to 256th IAP. On 8 February 121083 was transferred to 494th IAP, and the following August it joined 518th IAP and was assigned to Snr Lt Kasyanov (two Korean War victories). On 26 September the MiG was passed on to 676th IAP, where it was flown by Capts Shapovalov and Rebrov of 781st IAP until war's end.

24

MiG-15bis 123045 of Maj G F Dmitryuk, 821st IAP, Tatung-kao, April 1952

On 7 February 1952 this aircraft passed from 18th GvIAP to 821st IAP and was assigned to the regimental CO, HSU Maj Dmitryuk, who was to add five Korean War victories to the 18 he had scored during World War 2. On 3 May 1952, 123045 was transferred to 256th IAP and flown by Snr Lt Diyabelko, before being passed on to 676th IAP in August of that same year. Snr Lt Pozdnyakov successfully ejected from this aircraft when it was shot down during a dogfight with F-86s on 16 September 1952.

25

MiG-15bis 123051 of Maj A A Olenitsa, 821st IAP, Tatung-kao, July 1952

On 7 February 1952 18th GvIAP handed this aircraft over to 821st IAP, where it was assigned to assistant regimental CO, Maj Olenitsa (five Korean War victories). On 9 August 1952 the fighter was transferred to 878th IAP and flown by Capt Troshin (two Korean War victories). Snr Lt Ilin was its assigned pilot after 123051 joined 298th IAP in March 1953. By November 1954, when the aircraft was transferred to the Chinese Air Force, the venerable fighter had logged some 442 flying hours.

26

MiG-15bis 122033 of Maj V M Zabelin, 256th IAP, Dapu, early August 1952

Built by Factory No 1 in July 1950, this fighter served with a Soviet regiment in the Liaodong Peninsula prior to it being transferred to 18th GvIAP. Subsequently passed on to 821st IAP on 12 October 1951, 122033 was duly assigned to Capt Zabelin. Coinciding with his promotion to major in July 1952, Zabelin, who scored nine Korean War victories, was appointed deputy regimental CO of 256th IAP. When he moved to the latter regiment, Zabelin took this aircraft with him, but just weeks after his arrival at Dapu, 122033 was handed over to 676th IAP. Snr Lt Tatarov successfully ejected from the fighter when it was shot down in a dogfight with F-86s on 4 September 1952.

27

MiG-15bis 2315398 of Maj A S Boytsov, 16th IAP, Mukden-West, 12 June 1952

This aircraft is depicted as it appeared on the day 97th IAD command issued an order officially crediting Maj Boytsov with three kills, although the jet displays five victory stars. 97th IAD CO ordered the removal of the additional stars, noting that victory displays had to conform to divisional orders covering the crediting of pilots with official kills. But this order was never enforced, and by the time Arkadiy Boytsov had completed his tour of duty, the number of stars adorning this aircraft had risen to nine. Built by Factory No 153 in February 1952, 2315398 was subsequently delivered to 16th IAP and assigned to Boytsov (who ultimately achieved six Korean War victories) the following month. In August 1952 it was handed over to 913th IAP, and on 7 February 1953 the MiG-15 was shot down during a dogfight with Sabres whilst being flown by Lt Demyanov.

28

MiG-15bis 2415308 of Maj P V Minervin, 16th IAP, Mukden-West, May 1952

Built by Factory No 153 in February 1952, this aircraft was fielded by 16th IAP, 97th IAD and assigned to Maj Minervin (who scored three Korean War victories) in March 1952. Five months later it was handed over to 913th IAP, but on 23 May 1953 the fighter was shot down in a dogfight with F-86s. Its pilot, Capt Grishenchuk, was killed.

29

MiG-15bis 2915346 of Snr Lt Yuriy Dobrovichan, 147th GvIAP, Tatung-kao, 13 September 1952

This aircraft was built by Factory No 153 in July 1952 and delivered to 147th GvIAP, where it was assigned to the nightfighter squadron on 19 August. On 12 September 2915346 was used by Yuriy Dobrovichan to claim his first

Superfortress destroyed – by the turn of the year he had been credited with the destruction of two more. The aircraft was transferred to 37th IAD in August 1953 and to the Chinese Air Force in November 1954.

30

MiG-15bis 2115304 of Capt Vasiliy Lepikov, 415th IAP, Dapu, December 1952

Built by Factory No 153 in January 1952, this fighter was subsequently delivered to 415th IAP, 133rd IAD, which assigned it to Snr Lt (later Captain) Lepikov on 18 July 1952. Snr Lt Kuprin of the same regiment was shot down in 2115304 during a dogfight with F-86s on 29 May 1953.

31

MiG-15bis 2015363 of Capt N M Zameskin, 878th IAP, Tatung-kao, 4 February 1953

Nikolay Zameskin scored all six of his victories while flying this aircraft, with the last being claimed on 4 February 1953. The jet had been built by Factory No 153 in December 1951, delivered to 821st IAP in February 1952 and handed over to 878th IAP on 9 August. Assigned to Capt Zameskin, 2015363 was eventually replaced by a new MiG-15bis in April of the following year. Remaining with 878th IAP, however, the fighter was allocated to Capt Lomasov. Still in frontline service come war's end, 2015363 was handed over to 100th IAD in August 1953 and then transferred to the Chinese Air Force in November 1954.

32

MiG-15bis 53210546 of Capt Goncharov, 298th IAP, Tatung-kao, March 1953

Built by Factory No 21 at Gorkiy in October 1950, this aircraft did not reach 176th GvIAP until late 1951, as it had initially seen service with a Soviet unit based in the Liaodong Peninsula. In January 1952 53210546 was passed on to 148th GvIAP and in March to 351st IAP. The MiG joined 298th IAP in February 1953, whereupon it was assigned to Capt Goncharov. He was credited with destroying an enemy jet fighter (possibly a Skynight) in 53210546 on the night of 2 March. The aircraft was handed over to 100th IAD in June 1954 and then passed on to the Chinese Air Force five months later.

33

MiG-15bis 2315393 of Maj S A Fedorets, 913th IAP, Antung, 12 April 1953

This aircraft emerged from Novosibirsk's Factory No 153 in February 1952, entered service with one of 97th IAD's regiments the following month and was transferred to 913th IAP in August of that same year. There, 2315393 was assigned to Capt Fedorets, who scored five victories while flying it. All told, Semyon Fedorets achieved seven Korean War victories, and his fifth came during a dogfight with F-86s on 12 April 1953. Fedorets was shot down by Sabres later in the same engagement, although he managed to successfully eject from 2315393.

34

MiG-15bis 1915394 of Capt M I Mikhin, 518th IAP, Tatung-kao, June 1953

This aircraft was assigned to Mikhail Mikhin, who claimed nine victories with it. Built in December 1951 by Factory No 153, 1915394 was transferred to 415th IAP on 18 July 1952. In mid-August it was handed over to 518th IAP, and on the 17th the fighter was assigned to Mikhin – it remained his mount until war's end. In August 1953 the MiG was handed over to 100th IAD, who in turn passed it on to the Chinese Air Force in November 1954.

35

MiG-15bis 31530915 of Maj N M Zameskin, 878th IAP, Tatung-kao, June 1953

Built by Factory No 31 at Tbilisi in late 1952, this aircraft was fielded by 878th IAP the following February. In April it was assigned to Maj Zameskin, who continued to fly it until war's end. In August 1953 the fighter was handed over to the 100th IAD, who, in November 1954 transferred it to the Chinese Air Force.

36

MiG-15bis 2915316 of Maj S A Fedorets, 913th IAP, Antung, July 1953

Semyon Fedorets scored two victories while flying MiG-15bis 2915316, which was built by Factory No 153 in 1952. Assigned to the ace between May and July 1953, the fighter was handed over to 37th IAD the following month. During its time with the latter division, the jet was fitted with an ASP-4N gunsight and an SRD-1 radar range finder. 64th IAK transferred it to a 54th Air Army unit in November 1954.

─── ACKNOWLEDGEMENTS ───

The authors would like to extend their sincere appreciation to those who helped and supported them during the preparation of this work on the Korean War, namely E G Pepelyaev, A P Smorchkov, D A Samoylov, P V Minervin, M I Mikhin, N M Zameskin, N E Vorobyov, N M Chepelev, L N Ivanov, S A Fedorets, V N Shalfeev, V M Khvostantsev, L I Rusakov, B A Mukhin, N I Shkodin and many others, including those who have passed away. Thank you also to our wives for their immense patience. Photographs have been sourced from the Central Archive of the Ministry of Defence of Russia and the archives of E G Pepelyaev, A P Smorchkov, D A Samoylov, L N Ivanov, B A Mukhin, P V Minervin, N M Zameskin, M I Mikhin and N I Shkodin, as well as those of the authors.

INDEX

References to illustrations are shown in **bold**. Plates are shown with page and caption locators in brackets.